IT ONLY TAKES ONE

How to
Create the Right Idea—
And Then Make It Happen

John Emmerling

SIMON & SCHUSTER

NEW YORK   LONDON   TORONTO   SYDNEY   TOKYO   SINGAPORE

Simon & Schuster
Simon & Schuster Building
Rockefeller Center
1230 Avenue of the Americas
New York, New York 10020

DESIGNED BY BARBARA MARKS
Manufactured in
the United States of America

1   3   5   7   9   10   8   6   4   2

Library of Congress
Cataloging-in-Publication Data
Emmerling, John, date
It only takes one: how to create the right
idea and then make it happen/John
Emmerling.
p.   cm.
1. Creative thinking.   2. Success—
Psychological aspects.   3. Success in
business.   I. Title.
BF408.E45   1991
153.3'5—dc20   91-468
CIP
ISBN 0-671-72641-2

All illustrations are by the author except as noted below:

• Cartoon characters on page 30 from these strips (l. to r.):
"Luann," "Andy Capp," "Grin'n Bear It," "Hagar," "Beetle
Bailey," "Heathcliff," "Blondie." Photo by C. L. Chryslin

• Photos on pages 39 and 41 by Steven H. Begleiter

• Illustration on page 90 courtesy of U.S. Department of the
Interior, National Park Service, Edison National Historic Site

• Photo on page 136 by Joe Toto

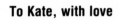

To Kate, with love

Table of Contents

Introduction

THE POWER OF AN IDEA

Who's creative? What's "being creative" all about? And if you could be *more* creative, *what good would it do you?*

Let's take these questions one at a time. Who's creative? When it comes to fresh, innovative thinking, the typical adult human brain is like a twelve-cylinder Ferrari that's been throttled back to idle, shifted into neutral, and left in a parking lot. You've got one of these "amazing machines," a mind capable of power, thrills, and acceleration. So are you creative? Yes—you've got all the basic equipment—but you may need some driver training.

What's "being creative" all about? Naturally, the very act of thinking up a new idea is creative. But this book will extend that concept one important step further. If there is to be a payoff, being creative—according to these pages—is coming up with a new idea and then *making that idea happen.*

Finally, what good will being more creative do you? Since idea-making can be learned, you can put creativity to work on the job generating nine-to-five ideas that open up new opportunities for your employer—and, of course, for you. Or you can use your newfound creative skills to think up ideas that switch on something exciting in your personal life. But is it going to be tough learning how to think up new ideas?

Nope. Like many things in life, idea-making is a process. And here's more good news for those of you who don't regularly invent totally new concepts like the automobile or the electric light bulb. There are *two kinds* of creativity. The first is what I call "Eureka Creativity," ideas that strike like thunderbolts, discoveries of original concepts that make a great leap forward. This kind of creativity is rare. After all, it takes incredible creative moxie to invent something like the steam engine. Or the airplane. Or nuclear energy. But, fortunately, Eureka Creativity makes up only a tiny percentage of total creativity. The overwhelmingly dominant kind of creativity is the second kind: "Nibble-Nibble Creativity."

Nibble-Nibble Creativity is looking at something and making it just a little bit better. Think of all the things produced by the joint efforts of every person alive. Think of the things you eat, touch, smell, look at, ride in, live in, and are entertained by—most of them are constantly being reinvented. Improved. Nibble by nibble. If you could zap forward a hundred years in a time machine, it's likely that most of the things you use today will have been improved. Some of the changes will result from great leaps (Eureka Creativity), but most of the products of the late twenty-first century will be the result of many small, innovative steps (Nibble-Nibble Creativity). And the nibble-nibble variety of idea-making is within the reach of everyone. Factory assembly line workers have become famous for their creative suggestions and small

innovations that cut costs, speed production, and enhance quality. Nibble-Nibble Creativity offers an opportunity for everyone to make significant contributions—and be recognized for them.

Do "Eureka" practitioners conjure something up out of nothing? Of course not. Almost all new ideas spring from stuff that came before. Often the "input" is just lying there, like ripe fruit waiting to be plucked. Thousands of years ago, the arch did not exist. No one knew a practical way to bridge a large gap with stones. Then (as I like to imagine it) there was a rockslide into a mountain gorge. By chance, the rocks tumbled into the narrow ravine and were wedged together in a peculiar way. A passage underneath the rocks just sort of happened—and courageous people and their donkeys were able to walk under this unwieldy structure. It's possible that such rockslide "accidents" happened hundreds of times the world over until finally a particularly creative human really looked at this overhead assemblage of stones and said, "Hmmmmm." Next came the leap. Eureka Creativity! "Maybe," he thought, "I could actually *arrange* stones across a gap." The result of this leap may have been an "arch" that looked something like this:

This first collection of rocks—a sort of hit-or-miss arrangement—was no doubt followed by dozens, possibly hundreds, who built better and better "arches." Somewhere along the line, another creative genius came along, figured out the principle of the keystone, the stone at the top, and the arch finally got to look like this:

After that the nibblers took over again and used the principle of the arch to build monuments, bridges, domed churches, aqueducts, and buildings galore.

■

While preparing this book, I interviewed a number of people who have the job of inspiring, encouraging, and directing creativity in large organizations. One of them was John Akers, chairman of IBM. I asked him if IBM is set up to foster creativity. "Absolutely," he said. "IBM spends seven billion dollars a year on research and development, and most of that is invested in creativity and innovation." He explained that IBM probably devotes a greater percentage of its R&D funds to the pursuit of "Eureka" creativity than any other industrial organization in the world. For example, one of the great "Eurekas" at IBM came in 1964. It was the System 360, the first family of computers that allowed all of a user's electronic boxes to "talk" to one another. The most recent IBM "Eureka" is the new superfast RISC, the Reduced Instruction Set Computer. This high-speed breakthrough was conjured up by Dr. John Cocke, one of IBM's band of geniuses who, within the company, have been dubbed "Wild Ducks."

So does that mean that the people who think up little ideas—the creative nibblers—are overlooked at IBM? Hardly. Akers spoke proudly of IBM's Corporate Technical Recognition Event. At this annual ceremony, technical people who have made significant creative contributions are invited, along with their spouses, to attend a multiday outing capped by a lavish dinner. On the big evening the lights are dimmed, spotlights come on, and Chairman Akers takes the podium to bestow honor and monetary rewards upon the fifty or so employees who have made incremental improvements in the product line. "Could I win, maybe, a $10,000 prize for some small idea?" I asked. "At IBM," Akers said, "I might hand you a $150,000 award for your nibble."

Big checks, of course, are nice. But the really thrilling thing about creativity is the tremor of excitement that emerges whenever a new little idea is born. "Hey, boss," you might say, "we've been using this two-page sales report for years. How about if I use our new size-reducing copier to make a miniature version of each page—and combine both pages on one sheet of paper?" The boss sparks to your idea and tells you to give it a try. You dub your new report "The Doubleheader," copies are distributed, and your fellow employees like the new compact presentation—while the environmentalists among them applaud your paper-saving concept and start calculating how many trees will be spared the chain saw. Then your boss walks up and says, "That 'Doubleheader' of yours was a crackerjack idea. Got any more brainstorms?" It's heady stuff. And you'll feel a warming glow impossible to extinguish. Because there is *nothing* that compares to coming up with a new idea and watching it succeed.

Once you learn how to generate ideas—and make them happen—you will find that the process gets easier and easier. The more you exercise your creativity, the more quickly new ideas will pop into your head. The more practice you get, the easier it is to push an idea forward enthusiastically and make it succeed. And then, of course, you get rewarded with more of that lushly addictive warming glow.

This book will take you through a six-step process called S.T.R.I.K.E., a simple way of looking at the mysteries of creating ideas and making them work. The acronym S.T.R.I.K.E. represents six powerful steps that will jumpstart your creative abilities. S.T.R.I.K.E. will start you thinking, give you a clear direction for your thoughts, help you develop an information base, demonstrate a visually oriented way to generate ideas, show you how to pick your single best idea, and finally encourage you to beat the drums, toot the horn, and actually make your new idea happen. After all, a brilliant—but *unused*—idea is a sorry, pitiful thing.

■

I'm in advertising. I've enjoyed a career of thinking up ideas for magazine ads and TV commercials, new ways to promote products, even new kinds of products themselves. In the pro-

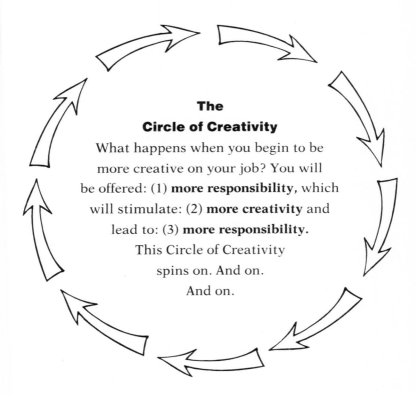

**The
Circle of Creativity**

What happens when you begin to be
more creative on your job? You will
be offered: (1) **more responsibility,** which
will stimulate: (2) **more creativity** and
lead to: (3) **more responsibility.**
This Circle of Creativity
spins on. And on.
And on.

cess I've listened to legions of marketing research gurus—the demographic and psychographic professionals who probe, study and analyze the consumers of America and then make educated guesses about the future course of our society. And they are all starting to say that the closing years of this century will be the time when "creativity" comes out of the closet. People with ideas—big ideas, medium ideas, little ideas—will become more prized and valued than ever.

Ideas are what can set you apart from the teeming masses. What might happen if (like the "Doubleheader" inventor) you start to be known on your job as someone who "always has a lot of good ideas"? Imagine yourself as the agile thinker who finds ways to solve new problems, the dynamo who conjures up innovative ways to deal with old problems. Ponder the magnificent possibilities if you are eventually dubbed the company wizard—the executive who can identify problems that nobody else realizes are problems, then come up with solutions that work. Of course, there are those who claim that "moving up in a corporation" robs you of your creativity, that responsibility stifles individual innovation. Poppycock! I've spent thirty years in business and have observed that it is the innovative thinkers who rise to the top—and then manage to stay there. The CEO of any major corporation is typically just as "creative" (*Definition:* Have an idea and make it happen) as any randomly selected artist, poet, or filmmaker. Fresh ideas—and the enthusiasm to make them happen—are the stuff of corporate victories.

■

Think about this: by the year 2000, this century will be history. The decade of the nineties is your last chance to make a dent in the twentieth century. You may not think so, but you have the ability to create changes that can improve your life. Take a look at the "Creative Wish List" that follows. Which of these wishes do you want to accomplish before the end of the century?

CREATIVE WISH LIST

- Do more original thinking on your job
- Invent or develop something new for your employer
- Be promoted to a position requiring creative ideas
- Switch to a more creative employer
- Change your career to something more creative
- Start your own company
- Sell something you've created
- Create an avocation that can earn you money
- Retire and start over at something brand new
- Become a sought-after expert
- Discover a creative ability you didn't know you had
- Use an existing tool (e.g., a computer, a camera, or a watercolor brush) in a totally new way
- Get some education in a whole new area
- Teach something valuable to children (or adults)

- Tackle your greatest fear
- Make something good happen in your community (something no one thought could happen)
- Undertake a project to benefit the world
- Accomplish an idea so big that your great-grandchildren will still be talking about it

Every one of those "wishes" requires that you first think up an idea. Then, once you've concocted your brainstorm, you'll move on to what will probably be the roughest, toughest, most challenging part of the creative process. Because ultimately you've got to tuck your brand-new concept under your arm, step out boldly into a cold, uncaring world, and make your idea *happen*.

This book will get you started on that rewarding road. I can't promise that you can make all your wishes come true. But I *can* promise you one thing. If you come up with an original idea and make it happen, you will be proud, happy, excited, thrilled, and incredibly turned on. You'll savor the experience. You'll relish that glow of good feeling about yourself, your job, and your life.

Then, of course, you'll begin working on your next idea.

PART I

Creative Tools
and Techniques

Chapter 1

FROM DUNCE TO DA VINCI— HOW CREATIVE ARE YOU?

Do you suffer from D.R.I.P.? It stands for a "Dearth of Robust Ideas and Plans." Do you have a dearth? How many new ideas—for your business or personal life—have you come up with this week? This month? In the past year? Jot down the best of them.

MY REALLY TERRIFIC IDEAS
(last 12 months)

(1) _____

(2) _____

(3) _____

(4) _____

(5) _____

How many did you come up with? If you listed two or three, you're an exception. Most people would probably feel blessed to list even one terrific idea. But the good news is, it only *takes* one.

Henry Ford took just one idea—assembly line production —and built automobiles cheaply enough for the masses to afford them. Putting that one idea to work changed Ford's life spectacularly. It also, of course, changed the world. Who was the Svengali who first twisted a bit of wire into the shape of a paper clip? Who wrote the most useful cookbook among those sitting on your kitchen shelf? What was the most innovative thing your employer accomplished in the past year? Who thought it up? (Incidentally, the answer is probably not "the engineering group" or "the marketing committee." In most cases, the truly good idea is conceived by a single individual—or a pair of individuals working as a team.) Whenever even one new idea is put into operation, *change happens.* And if you are the one who comes up with that idea, the change will bring with it a flood of positive benefits.

Okay, be honest now. How creative are you? Most people have a general idea of how "smart" they are. Somewhere along the line a teacher probably leaked your supposedly confidential IQ score and revealed that you are a 115 or a 127 or maybe even a superstar of 150 or above. But is a high IQ score a sign of high "creativity"? Not necessarily. High creativity thrives on the somewhat oddball ability to see things differently—and then spot new connections in the old stuff. Most new ideas are the result of cross-fertilization between previously unrelated thoughts.

In the mid-1400s, Johannes Gutenberg spent years trying to invent a way to make duplicate copies of documents easily. The monks who painstakingly handprinted parchment sheets one at a time must have seemed awfully inefficient to Gutenberg. So he thought about: (1) the paper rubbings that reproduced pictures etched on stones. He thought about: (2) the metal coin punch used to strike an image on individual coins. And he thought about: (3) the wine screw press that put a slow, steady pressure on a surface. Then one day he put it all together—Eureka!—and came up with a stunning idea. Gutenberg carved each letter of the alphabet on its own little "coin punch." Next, he arranged a series of the punches to form words and locked them into position with a wooden frame. Finally, he inked his type punches, put a sheet of paper underneath the rig, and applied slow, steady pressure with a wine press. When he unscrewed the press and withdrew the sheet of paper, he was looking at the world's first printed document. Gutenberg's "printing press"—with its movable type—was a wondrous machine that revolutionized the way people communicated. Yet it was simply a unique, innovative way of arranging familiar elements.

The mind's ability to jump, cross-fertilize, mix, and blend (as Gutenberg's mind did) is truly incredible—but those abilities are not measured by a standard IQ test. So let's invent our own measure of creativity. It's a simple line graph that will help you visualize your "Creativity Quotient," or CQ.

```
L_____._____J
```

DUNCE   DA VINCI

At the left of the graph is DUNCE—the dullest person you can conjure up. A DUNCE is someone who, when first asked to boil an egg, can't find the stove. The DUNCE is a "never ever." He has never ever had an original thought or idea. He has never ever broken a rule and follows them rigorously his entire life. Lead him to the stove and show him how to boil an egg, and he will never vary the routine by one iota. It is inconceivable to imagine that the true DUNCE, with egg in hand, would *ever* think of scrambling it.

Now, way over on the right side of the graph is DA VINCI. Leonardo da Vinci gets my vote as the world's most original and innovative idea-maker to date. Born in Italy during the Renaissance, Leonardo produced paintings, such as his enigmatic *La Gioconda* ("Mona Lisa") that rivaled the best of the Old Masters. But his mind stretched much further. He was also a sculptor, an architect, a city planner, a mathematician, a scientist, and a prolific inventor of such amazing things as chain links, a spring-driven car, the parachute, and the helicopter. To entertain the court occasionally, he became a singer and a lute player. And to appease the warlike, he designed concepts for shrapnel bombs, battle tanks, and a crude forerunner of the machine gun.

The little mark in the middle of the graph is the halfway point between DUNCE and DA VINCI. It represents a middle-of-the-road average for "creativity." Now, let's figure out where *you* are on that line. There's no test to take. You simply make a mark where you think you are, relative to all the people you work with, play with, live with, and compete with. Chances are, your mark will fall on the right side of the graph, more DA VINCI than DUNCE.

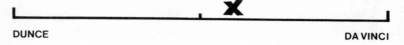

DUNCE   **DA VINCI**

In other words, you think you have the potential for creative thinking, but you've probably never made a concerted effort to *improve* your CQ. As you begin to focus on the creative process, however, you'll discover that there are some simple steps you can take that will move your mark further to the right.

Do you want to generate more new ideas, and then—one idea at a time—make them happen? Do you want more of that elusive quality described enviously as "creativity"? Do you truly want to nudge your X toward the far right side of the scale? If you just answered yes, yes, and yes, the first thing you have to do is turn on the creativity you already have, just waiting to be tapped. And before long that D.R.I.P. will become a gusher.

Chapter 2

LOOSENING UP—A FEELING YOU'LL NEVER FORGET

As you probably know, the left hemisphere of the human brain controls your rational, sequential, linguistic functions. It's very good at precise logical things like math and science. (Think of the left brain as TIGHT.) The right hemisphere is emotional, visual, intuitive—and imaginative. It is free-spirited and perceptive enough to see both the forest *and* the trees. (Think of the right brain as LOOSE.) Most people agree that true creativity—the ability to see things differently, or put them together in different ways—originates in the right hemisphere. But first you may have to trick your hidebound left brain into giving your fun-loving right brain more sway.

Wouldn't it be exciting to break some of those left-brain rules you've always lived by—to start to look at things *differently?* The USSR—of all places—may have a lesson for us. As reported in *Fortune* magazine, there are now "creative development" seminars for Soviet citizens, an experiment initiated under Premier Mikhail Gorbachev's policy of *perestroika.* Aimed at government officials and factory workers, these seminars include one piece of advice intended to loosen up a hidebound citizen's view of life: "Don't get stuck in confining routines. For variety, when you go to your home tonight don't enter through the door. Instead, *try going in through the window."*

The very act of doing something in a totally new way upsets your left brain's applecart and you suddenly discover the joy of an unexpected viewpoint. You edge back toward that time long ago when your left brain was a blank slate. Think about it. We make our debut on this planet as seven or eight pounds of totally free spirit. At the moment of birth, there are no no's, no constraints. It is a time of incredible freedom that goes on for several weeks, possibly even several months. But then our parental drill sergeants start to issue orders. They initiate construction of the little boxes we will be asked to live in. More little boxes pile up with a thunderous acceleration as the years go by. There are educational demands, religious codes of conduct, employment obligations, social and legal requirements, the demands of relationships, and so on. Most of us live lives that are tightly confined by an astounding number of boxes. So start by jumping out of a couple of them. Open yourself to the power of new perceptions and ideas—then put them to work to make positive changes in your life. Oliver Wendell Holmes put it this way:

> **"Man's mind stretched by a new idea never goes back to its original dimension."**

Here are some loosening-up exercises that will stretch your mind and give you a new perspective on old habits and familiar activities. Read the following list of suggestions and pick three or four of them to try. You'll find that you will experience, or see, familiar things in unfamiliar ways. Your left brain will be grasping to find "logic" in your actions. Your right brain will be having a ball.

(1) Switch your watch to your other wrist for a whole day. (Will anyone else notice? No. Will you notice? Every single time you glance at your nude wrist.)

(2) Try an obscure candy bar you've never tasted. Eat just one bite and write a ten-word description of it. (Ever notice how tough it is to describe a taste?)

(3) Cut some squares, circles, and triangles out of colored paper and move the pieces around until they make a picture. How many different pictures can you make?

(Man reading newspaper)

Before   **After**

(4) Rearrange your life's places. Move your bed to another spot. Switch the TV to another position. If you work in an office and your desk faces a door, turn it so it faces a window or a wall. How do these feel? Do any of the new arrangements work better?

(5) Using dabs of glue, build a six-foot tower of empty soda pop cans. Be eclectic in your choice of brands and in the arrangement of cans. Don't take more than thirty minutes making it. Now lean your "pop art" tower against a wall and observe how quickly it seizes the attention of all who enter.

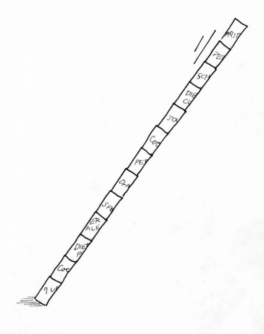

(6) At night, take the shades off your living room lamps and, if you have them, install some bright, high-wattage bulbs. Then stand back and take a look at a very different room. (Where did all those cracks come from?)

(7) Own a food processor? Thoroughly blend together one fruit and one vegetable. Taste the mixture and pretend it is a product you are going to sell. What will you name it? (For example, a mixture of crushed grapes and butternut squash might be called "Squish-Squash.")

(8) Put your hand on a copier machine and make a series of unusual poses, from graceful to grotesque. Study them closely. What other forms and images do they suggest?

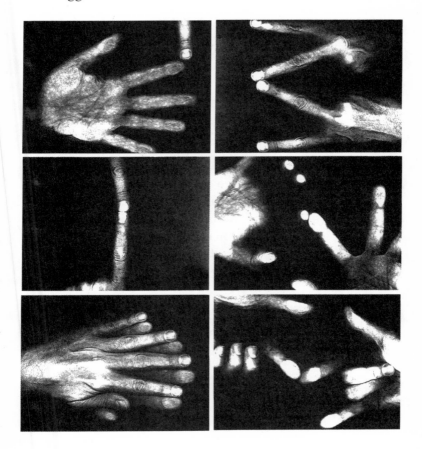

(9) If you have a video camcorder, slither through your home on your belly pointing the lens up at the underside of tables—underneath and around chairs, appliances, and beds. When you view the tape, this "snake's-eye view" will show an unfamiliar place you've never seen.

(10) Upset your day's routine. Do you always start your day with a shower? Tomorrow, start with a bath. Do you

always finish your day with the same 11 P.M. television news show? Tomorrow, switch to another channel's news show.

(11) If you are right-handed, copy the following line using your left hand (vice versa for lefties).

If my life began to unravel, would I write like this?

If my lif began to unravel, would I write like this?

(12) Take a pair of scissors to the comic section of the newspaper and clip out various cartoon characters. Tape them to a sheet of paper in a montage—a "social gathering" of famous cartoon characters. For spice, toss in a photo of a public figure. Is there a caption you can add to give it some zing?

As you did these loosening-up exercises, you were *going in through the window*, jumping out of boxes. You were break-

ing molds and forcing your brain to stray from familiar paths. You were seeing yourself, your routine habits, and your familiar surroundings in different ways. How did it feel? Were you surprised, confused, intrigued, a little uncomfortable—all of the above? These are the feelings you'll get when you try something new—and this is only the beginning.

There is more to come. Lots more.

Chapter 3

"HELLO THERE, RIGHT SIDE OF BRAIN"

Your primary creative tool is the right hemisphere of your brain. It "sees" things. But you have to let it do its thing. Unfortunately, your straitlaced martinet of a left brain has been working hard since childhood to restrict your right brain's ability to really see. Here's a little test. Look at the shapes below and try to make some sense out of them.

Some people (those with fast, loose right brains) will spot the answer immediately. Others may require espionage to decipher this message. (NOTE: I just gave your left brain a clue.)

If you're having trouble with this, you're obeying left-brain rules that insist you look only at positive defined objects and try to figure out their "logic." Try something different. Loosen up and focus on the negative, undefined spaces *between* the positive objects. Can you spot the word "SPY"? If you're still having problems, look at the figure below in which the negative spaces are now defined. Got it? Now it will probably be difficult to look at the figures without seeing "SPY." Your right brain has just broken a couple of your left brain's steel bands.

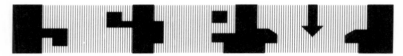

After years of developing television commercials, I've learned that the quickest path to getting someone to understand a message is to make it visual. If you can see something, it has a way of sticking in your mind, never to be forgotten. Memory courses, for example, work this way. Years ago I took one of those classes where we were taught how to remember the names of the thirty people taking the course.

"Emmerling," the instructor suggested when he came to me. "Why doesn't everyone here picture John standing up with a goofy grin and wearing a giant emerald ring on his head. Once you have that picture in your head, I challenge you to forget John Emeraldring's name." I took that memory course twenty years ago, but I still occasionally run into someone on the street who was in the class. Often, I can still remember the person's name. And he remembers the guy with the weird ring on his head. Such is the power of a visual idea.

As a teenager I entered college to study architecture. But in my spare time I began to explore cartooning as an alternative career. I taught myself to sketch and began to look at the world around me for ideas. If I saw or imagined something odd or slightly amusing, I drew it and then tried to find the unique twist that would make it a belly laugh. What caption would work with what picture to create the "unexpected juxtaposition" that makes us guffaw? I figured that if a cartoon I scribbled could make me smile, it was worth taking ten minutes to do the finished rough sketch and letter in the caption. Every week I mailed batches of a dozen cartoons each to my favorite publications. Each morning, I eagerly searched my mail for the big check I was certain would be coming. After several months, however, a frank accounting revealed that I would not soon be driving a brand-new '58 Corvette. My collection of rejection notes and encouraging little "Stick with it" messages was growing to an impressive height. Although I did sell a couple of my cartoons (highest sale: $50), my earning potential seemed close to zilch. But I had developed an ability to sketch quickly and

"I thought I'd take a break."

A first cartoon is published (age 19).

capture the essence of a situation—to visualize an idea. It is an ability that for years has allowed me to have a "visual view" of problem solving. It is a technique that speaks to the core of creativity. Visuals are the lubricant that makes high-grade ideas flow.

Let me share this bit of magic with you—a simple way to add visual input to your thinking process. Get ready to become a "cartoonist." All you need is a pen and some paper. Or, if you want to go first class, gather up the things listed below—a couple of these items may already be on your desk or sitting in a kitchen drawer. Your local stationery or art supply store will have the rest.

(1) A thick, black art marker (to make thick lines)
(2) A black felt-tip pen (for thin lines)
(3) A bottle of black ink
(4) One 14" × 17" pad of drawing paper

Begin by thinking back. Remember when you first started drawing—a house, a sailboat, a tree? There may not have been much resemblance between your drawing and the real thing—except in your eyes. The first human beings you drew were probably stick figures: straight lines for the arms and legs, a circle for the head. Again, there may have been no resemblance, but you were *visualizing* yourself or another person. And when you put shapes and stick figures together, you were visualizing a scene or a situation. You were even visualizing your ideas and feelings by the way you drew these shapes and figures. After that, your visual reservoir probably began to dry up. So let's fill it again—with a combination of pictures and words I call "Fingertoons."

Start by using a pen or your thick black marker to make a box on a blank sheet of paper. Now place two fingers of your left hand in the box and trace the outline of the tops of each finger with the thin felt-tip pen. (NOTE TO LEFTIES: If it's easier to trace your right hand, reverse the instructions.) Take a good look at the two unusual shapes that follow:

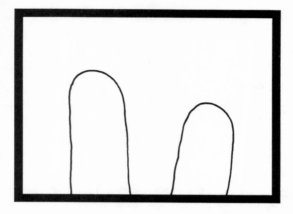

What do these outlines suggest to you? How about a man—the taller outline—and a woman—the shorter one? All you have to do is add a few simple lines, dots, and curls to bring your figures to life. Like this:

Slightly amusing, yes. You've visualized two people, but you haven't yet visualized a scene or a situation. So let's move on to adding captions. In the illustration above, the figure on the left looks sort of dumb and trusting (it's all in the eyes and mouth). The figure on the right seems set to deliver a snappy rejoinder (once again, eyes and mouth do the trick). So let's give Mr. Dumb and Trusting a question to ask and Ms. Snappy Rejoinder a little spear to toss at him. Something like this:

You can write your own dialogue for these two little figures. Or get things started with the "Fingertoon Linefinder" that follows. Look over the five questions in List A and pick your favorite as a caption for the figure on the left. Then go to List B for a response. You'll find several responses for each question, some funnier or more unexpected than others. (EX-AMPLE: To the question "What's for dinner?" you could answer "Banana pudding," "Your pet goat," or "A bag of rotten avocados." But the response "How about the piano?" might be more amusing.)

THE FINGERTOON LINEFINDER

List A
What's for dinner?
Who left these socks?
What's this mess?
Why are you leaving me?
What can make you happy?

List B
Banana pudding.
Your pet goat.
Check with Nancy Reagan.
How about the piano?
A bag of rotten avocados.
The New York Yankees.
I'd have to write a thesis.
Ask the mailman.
I'm taking the Fifth.

You're now equipped with the basics. You can draw little figures and add any captions that strike your fancy. Try a few Fingertoons of your own. Reverse the man and woman figures. Add a child by using your little finger. For an imposing "authority figure," experiment with tracing your thumb. Vary the facial expressions to suggest different scenes and situations. Then begin composing your own questions and offbeat responses. Your left brain may respond by saying to you: "This *visual* stuff isn't what I usually do—but I like it."

■

Today, whether it's a business or personal problem, if I want to grab hold of it, I draw a picture of it. Here's how this trick works. Make a Fingertoon of yourself and add a specific caption by writing a few words that describe a problem you want to fix, an idea or opinion you have, or an opportunity you want to grab. Let's say you're concerned about scheduling your business tasks more efficiently. You might "bring that problem to life" by making a Fingertoon something like this:

Drawing a picture does something that is incredibly powerful. It "programs" the visual, creative, intuitive right side of your brain to understand where you're heading. Your goal is now quickly accessible for review by a glance at your picture—or by simply calling up its mental image. Unburdened

by the laborious, wordy narratives that are fodder for the left brain, you will have a quick reference point. About to make a decision—but you'd like to make sure it's appropriate to reaching your goal? Call up that visual image. Let the right side of your brain show you how it feels. At the risk of going overboard on this point, I really believe that this kind of visualization on a sheet of paper becomes:

THE WORLD'S MOST POWERFUL SHEET OF PAPER

Want to make a graphic that might work even better than your Fingertoon? Here's another way to visualize a problem or a goal—a signpost with dynamic power and undeniable realism.

Select an expendable photograph of yourself and cut out your figure with scissors. Now place the cutout on a copying machine (if it's an enlarging copier, try making yourself about six inches high). With your image now emblazoned on an 8½″ × 11″ sheet of white paper, take a 50-cent piece and trace a caption balloon (don't forget the little pointer). Run off a bunch of copies of you and your empty balloon. Then, in the caption balloon, letter in a brief statement of your particular problem or goal. Limit yourself to less than ten words; the briefer, the better. Tape the picture to your refrigerator or to your office wall, or fold it up and keep it in your pocket or purse—and let it work its magic.

It will.

Here's how visualizing can help in another way. And you won't have to draw pictures or cut up family photos. Whenever I stand up to give an important presentation, deliver a speech, or even present a toast at a birthday party, I am doing it for the third or fourth time because I have previously visualized it. The idea of treating an important audience to a stumbling first blurt-out of my ideas strikes me as foolhardy. Would you open your new play on Broadway without first trying it out in the sticks? I hope not.

I've worked in the past with Marshall Loeb, the award-winning managing editor of *Fortune* magazine. Loeb's career has revolved around the reporting, writing, and editing of words—and his constant search for fascinating and explanatory pictures. His graphic sense is keen (read: agile right brain) and it comes into play in many ways. I've been in auditoriums with him during the few minutes before a sizable audience gathers to hear him speak. There is no talking to Marshall during these moments. He paces the empty hall, murmuring to himself, making subtle gestures, and only occasionally glancing at his text. He is "running a movie" of Marshall Loeb in front of this audience delivering this speech. He is not sitting in a quiet corner calmly studying words from a script. He's in action—picturing himself at the podium delivering his words, reacting to the audience, emphasizing certain phrases with gestures, and then succinctly answering the questions he expects will be asked. The speech, it goes without saying, is always a success. He makes it seem so easy. And it *is* easy because of the visual workout that has prepared him for a smooth, effective presentation.

The most productive impetus to creativity—whether you're trying to come up with a new idea or to solve problems —is to call on the visual right side of your brain. Fingertoons, captioned photographs, mental rehearsals of what you want to accomplish, all will stimulate your creative thinking because you have a "picture" of your objective in your mind. While your left brain is telling you it can't be done, your right brain is busy trying to figure out ways it *can* be done. I have a friend who, when he first started out in business, conjured up an image of himself behind the wheel of a Porsche 911. His left brain said, "Forget it. Settle for a Chevrolet." But my friend couldn't repress that powerful picture of himself. Naturally, he finally got the Porsche—and he felt right at home.

The moral to that story: If you can "see" where you want to go, you can probably figure out a way to get there.

Chapter 4

GOOD RULES, BAD RULES, AND CHANGING THE RULES

Think about the world of a very small child named Julie. Julie is a few months old and has been relatively unburdened so far by the rules of those monster adults looming about her. One day, Julie's little hand manages to grasp a small ball and pick it up. She looks at it quizzically (*"What is this thing attached to my hand?"*). Then, accidentally, she relaxes her fingers a bit. The thing leaves her hand immediately, falling to the floor of her playpen (*"What in the world just happened?"*). She grasps at the ball, watching it again attach itself to her hand (*"Will it go away again?"*). Slowly she unfurls her fingers. It drops. And she is filled with excitement. Author and child psychologist Dr. Lee Salk has observed this phenomenon many times and describes it as the child experiencing "a feeling of WOW." Julie has just invented—for herself—the concept of gravity.

Think about those first two years of your life. Sure, you got some input from adults. But so much other stuff was coming at you from the physical environment. Every day, you bumped into new things, stumbled into new experiences. And every time you did something, discovered something, you were doing it for the first time. You really were—for yourself—inventing the universe. Your little brain was yelping out a stream of excited reactions—"Wow!" "Wow!" "Wow!" It was a rollicking good time of incessant discovery. But all too soon you also discovered "The Rules"—things you're supposed to do and *not* do—because somebody says so.

So what about rules? Are they creativity killers for little kids (and big adults)? Let's take a look at the "crayon rules." Hand a box of colorful crayons to a little tyke who has never seen such a thing and watch what happens. He may dump them out and throw the crayons around. He may try to eat the purple crayon. He may discard all the crayons and play with the box. He may even—to his joy—discover that crayons make beautiful marks on paper (and walls) and happily begin to scribble the kind of art that can make parents swoon. The point is, he doesn't know what he is *supposed* to do with crayons—or what he *isn't* supposed to do with them. So he plays. He experiments. He does odd things with them. And he allows some delightful accidents to happen.

Little children are blessed in that they do not suffer from that perverse, universal, adult-imposed creativity squasher, "fear of looking stupid." They just playfully move ahead, allowing whatever happens to happen, until cautious parents impose some rules to exert control over their infant Picasso. With luck these enlightened dictators will impose *good crayon rules* and not *bad crayon rules*.

> GOOD CRAYON RULE: Don't draw on the walls.
> BAD CRAYON RULE: You must use the red crayon
>   to draw an apple.

Naturally, good rules are those that provide constructive guidance, without exerting an iron-clamp control over creativity. And in a truly creative home, a child will always test those rules and know how to change them if they suddenly cease to apply.

MOM: "A workman is coming tomorrow to wallpaper this room."

CHILD: "Can I draw on the walls today?"

God bless Mom if she says yes.

Do Rules Inspire or Inhibit Creativity?

Stephen Sondheim is certainly one of the most creative songwriters ever to prowl the talent-consuming world of Broadway. His credits as a lyricist and composer include dozens of musical blockbusters like *West Side Story, Company,* and *Sweeney Todd.* So it must be easy for Sondheim to whip out a love song, right?

Well, yes. And no.

I had the opportunity to ask Sondheim how he thought up song ideas. He responded by saying that if someone asked him to "write a love song" and handed him a blank sheet of paper, he'd be at a complete loss. However, when he starts out to write a love song based on *a specific scenario*, it opens up creative options. He described an example of what a play's author might say to him to get him started on a song. "Picture this," he said. "It's three A.M. and a woman is sitting alone in a dark empty bar. She's on her fourth martini and is thinking about the man who just left her . . ." Writing that song, according to Sondheim, is easier because the situation "sets the rules." Within those rules he will create a hauntingly romantic song about a woman you will care very much about. You will never have heard a song anything like it; the song may move you tremendously. But it will have followed the rules.

There is a common misperception: "Innovation thrives best in a totally uninhibited, unencumbered environment." In fact, the opposite is usually true. Rules tend to inspire creativity because they set the boundaries—and then permit more intensive exploration within them. Rollo May, in his 1975 book *The Courage to Create*, writes about ". . . the phenomenon that *creativity itself requires limits,* for the creative act arises out of the struggle of human beings with and against that which limits them." Turning to the world of music, May describes asking Duke Ellington how he created his musical compositions. The Duke explained that since his trumpet player could reach certain notes beautifully but not other notes, and the same was true of his trombonist, he had to write his music within those limits. "It's good to have limits," Ellington said.

Speaking of rules, restrictions, and limits, how about the game of football? This contest is played on a field with carefully specified sidelines and goal lines. There is a comprehensive rule book that goes on for page after page detailing what can and cannot be done. At game time, a bunch of uniformed officials prance around the field making sure each team lives up to the letter of the law. As an environment for creativity, doesn't that sound restrictive, constrained, and stultifying? Hardly. Talk to a hundred coaches and each will tell you at length how he manages to be cunning, crafty, and sometimes wildly creative within those rules and boundaries. There *is* creativity in football. There *is* creativity in the tightly defined world of business. And there *is* creativity available to you in your personal life.

Most experts agree that it is the left brain that sets the rules: "This is the way it *should* be done. This is the way it's *always* been done. This is the *only* way it can be done." Such rules can be a lead weight on the playful, experimental impulses of the right brain, inhibiting creativity. *Or* they can be a challenge.

Here's an exercise in being creative within rules. In this case, the "rules" are a wonderfully unpredictable form—the inkblot. Drop a large globule of black ink onto a sheet of paper and splat it with another sheet of paper. Now look at your strangely shaped blot. What does it suggest to you and how can you transform that blot into a visual image by adding just a subtle line, dot, or feature here or there? What words could you use to caption that image? These are your rules: Start with an ink blot, transform it into an image, and make a "Blotski." Here's an example to inspire you:

THE BLOT

THE BLOTSKI

MOSQUITO
CONFRONTS THE
BIG BAD WOLF

Remember, this isn't a Rorschach test. Instead of limiting your imagination to the blot itself ("Tell me, vat do you see in zis little blot?"), go ahead and add some creative features of your own. Don't limit yourself to looking at your inkblot just one way. Rotate it. Look at it from all angles. Let your mind run off in as many directions as that blob of ink did. Almost any little blot can be transformed into an image when seen from a fresh point of view (notice that the "wolf" Blotski has been turned 90 degrees counterclockwise from its original position):

Here are three more blots. How would you turn them into Blotskis? Come up with a solution of your own for each blot.

THREE BLOTS

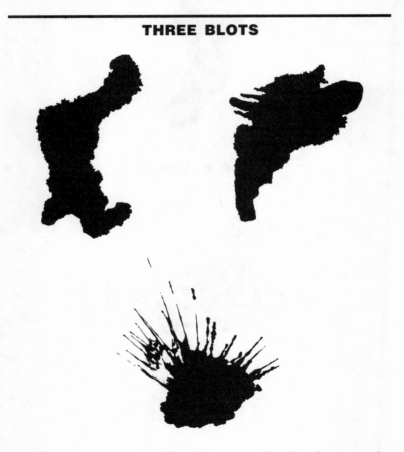

Then compare your Blotskis to my Blotskis shown at the end of this chapter—only three modest visualizations out of at least seven zillion possibilities.

How about creativity—and rules—in business? The demands of a competitive marketplace require that commercial innovation always work within some set of rules. That is the challenge of any creative assignment. Imagine a company founded in the 1920s and dedicated to providing customers with the most innovative toiletry products the owner and his managers can think up. In a moment of nautical inspiration, the owner dubs the company "Sailor Boy." It is his decree that all of their new soaps, shaving creams, colognes, and mustache waxes will carry the proud "Sailor Boy" brand name. Fortunately, the company launches a couple of good products and immediately sets sail profitably. But sprinkled among their successes, a couple of wacky ideas are proposed. For example, the response to their flower-scented aftershave is lousy; it turns out that men don't particularly want to smell like lilacs. So the owner then does what all owners do when they start to lose some money here and there. He makes some rules about new Sailor Boy products. And in this case, they're pretty good rules:

RULES FOR NEW "SAILOR BOY" PRODUCTS

(1) It must cost less than 5 cents to make.
(2) It must sell for more than 50 cents.
(3) Customers must like it.
(4) It must get used up quickly.

Back in the twenties, you could probably have built a major American toiletries company by heeding those rules— and demanding that every new product idea meet those four tests. Rather than inhibiting the creative process, the founder's four rules would probably spur employees to greater flights of imagination.

But rules aren't made in a vacuum. As times and circumstances change, the marketplace adapts to them and the rules must also be changed. If not, good rules can quickly become bad rules and instead of inspiring creativity, they stifle it. For example, let's say we're back in the 1940s and you're a talented young executive just starting a career with Sailor Boy. Now in business for twenty years, the company has achieved incredible success. Many of its products are number one in their categories and the founder's four rules have been engraved in stone. Your boss thinks you're an eager beaver and has assigned you to new product development. Of course, the company rules have been adjusted for inflation. Rule 1 now allows product cost to reach 10 cents and Rule 2 now requires that your product sell for more than one dollar. All else remains the same.

Your boss turns you loose in the shaving cream category, where your company has much earlier pioneered the idea of taking shaving soap out of the shaving mug and putting it, in *liquid* form, into a handy tube. Sailor Boy tube shaving cream is doing just great: It's number one in the market with a 48 percent share of the tube shaving cream category. How in the world are you going to top that? You stew. You talk to store managers. You surround yourself with tubes. And you think very, very hard. Then one day your wife comes home from the hardware store with a newfangled can of bug spray. It has some sort of gas in it so that the insecticide sprays out in a fine mist when a little button is pushed. You start to think. Bug spray . . . gas . . . push button . . . shaving cream . . . gas . . . push button . . . Suddenly an idea strikes: What if we made push-button shaving cream?

Eagerly, you contact the manufacturer of the bug spray can to find out how the spray mechanism is made and how much it costs. Bad news. The device costs at least 15 cents to manufacture. To that you will also have to add the cost of soap, can, and packaging. Obviously, the rule that requires that all products must cost less than 10 cents to make has just become an *incredibly bad* rule. If Sailor Boy insists on maintaining the "10-cent cost" formula, the firm will miss the opportunity to create the aerosol shaving cream category —the chance to be both innovator and share leader in a new product form. What is at stake may be the difference between climbing to a 40 or 50 percent share as the first entry in a hot new category or sinking to a minuscule sales level as your outmoded, dusty tubes are shoved to the back of drugstore shelves.

But your fellow executives will understand this instantly and change the rules—right? Not necessarily. Depending on the entrenched strength of the people defending those rules, you may have a really tough battle ahead. To cite another example of good rules gone bad, soon after World War I ended, a group of powerful naval officers argued long and hard that aircraft carriers were a foolish and frivolous concept, and that it should be obvious to any person of reasonable intelligence that battleships were the answer to all future challenges of naval warfare. The airplane itself was simply a little toy sometimes useful for aerial scouting or carrying the mail. Some of those hidebound thinkers continued to hold on to their opinions until one sunny Sunday morning in December of 1941 when the Japanese sunk a big chunk of the American fleet—and did it with "little toy airplanes" launched from aircraft carriers.

The ability to recognize when good rules have become bad ones—and the foresight, intelligence, and imagination to change them—is the hallmark of true creativity. Here's an example. T. Vincent Learson spent his entire career at IBM, progressing from a beginning sales job to become the first chairman of the company not blessed with the last name of Watson. A six-foot, five-inch, booming-voiced decision maker, Learson was not the sort of person prone to sit around meekly following rules. By 1954, he had taken charge of engineering, manufacturing, and sales for all IBM computers. However, the company's leading computer, the IBM 702, was plagued with problems and Learson championed a decision to withdraw it from the market. ("It wasn't a very good machine," he recalled in a recent interview.) *The New York Times* pounced on this story and declared that apparently IBM was dropping out of the computer business. No doubt the executives at IBM's fierce competitor, the UNIVAC company, were delighted, rubbed their hands in glee, and redoubled their efforts to sell UNIVAC computers. Immediately, precious time began to slip away. IBM's "computer gap" could not be allowed to continue for a number of months. Learson led a crash engineering project that, in the remarkable span of three months, developed the IBM 705, a significantly better computer than the recently dumped 702. Now he had to sell a large, high-profile customer and reestablish the IBM reputation. The 705, which was invented but not yet *manufactured*, would be the key.

Fortunately there was a big, ripe customer shopping in the marketplace. Out in Chicago, the huge Commonwealth Edison utility company had asked both UNIVAC and IBM to bid on satisfying their computer needs. And the growing world of computer users was watching this contest with keen interest. Learson went to Chicago and pitched the account personally. The Commonwealth Edison people thought the 705 sounded like a good, possibly even superior, machine. But the utility's board of directors had a little problem: "We'll be able to save $50,000 a month with your new machine, Mr. Learson. But if you deliver late, will IBM pay a penalty of $50,000 a month?"

Back at IBM headquarters in New York City, Thomas Watson, Sr., the founder of the company (and the author of the company's longtime slogan, "Think") was very much running the show. The "Old Man" was as tough as nails—and he had established some very strict rules. One of them: "IBM does not pay penalties." A companion rule: "Anyone who allows a change in the standard contract is automatically subject to being fired." Employees were not expected to *think* about those two rules—just obey them. But on the spot in Edison's Chicago offices, Learson did not hesitate when asked about the penalty. He did not request the opportunity to "sleep on it." He did not ask for a minute to call the home office. He simply said, "Yes, sir, we'll accept that penalty— and we'll write it into the contract." Commonwealth Edison agreed to the IBM proposal. Learson signed and then returned to New York to face the music. This is how the lyrics went:

THOMAS WATSON, SR.:   "What about this penalty?"

LEARSON: "It was *absolutely essential* to the deal, Mr. Watson. This is the number one account in the country—and the whole country is watching to see which way it goes."

WATSON: "I think you did the right thing. Thank you very much."

P.S. Learson's manufacturing team pulled it off and got a brand-new IBM 705 installed in Chicago on time. The company never paid a nickel of penalty.

Truly creative people usually do their best work within a set of rules. But there are good rules (the ones that are still sharply relevant) and bad rules (the ones that have gone out of whack). If you can spot those off-kilter rules and then muster up sufficient creative gumption to propose new ideas for old assumptions, new solutions for old problems, you can be a person who brings energy and innovation to your job, your community, and your personal life. So now that you have loosened up to do things a little differently, now that you know how to think visually, and now that you have honed your understanding of what rules are—and are not—it's time to move on to the process of creating new ideas and making them happen.

It is now time to S.T.R.I.K.E.

THREE BLOTSKIS

BEAR WITH
BAG ON HEAD

POPEYE
STICKING HEAD
OUT WINDOW

HOW TO FRIGHTEN
A PORCUPINE

PART II

S.T.R.I.K.E.

How to
Increase
Your Creativity

Chapter 5

THE DREADED
BLANK SHEET OF PAPER

(1) How could you have said something that dumb to her? You're back at your place now, it's after midnight, and you know she's still awake. And very angry. You don't want to call; that will just start the argument all over again. So you decide to write a note and drop it off at her door in the morning. You reach for a pen and a blank piece of paper.

You stare at the paper. It stares back at you. And nothing happens.

(2) "We'll meet at three this afternoon," your boss said earlier today. "Bring along all your ideas on how to open up the new sales territory in Minnesota. Oh, and I'd like them in a written memo." You do have a couple of half-formed

thoughts—and would have been far more comfortable just winging them at the meeting—but now you need to put them in writing. Your ideas need to be specific and understandable. You take out a blank piece of paper.

You stare at the paper. It stares back at you. And nothing happens.

(3) So far, you've got an A in this course. The book reports you've turned in have been well-written summaries of the assigned novels. But the teacher pulled a fast one today. "Let's pretend *you* are the novelist," she said, "and on Monday I'd like you to turn in a two-page outline of a new novel you are working on." What in the world should you write about? You've been asking yourself this question for several hours now. There are seven crumpled sheets of paper—clumsy, false-sounding attempts—in your wastepaper basket. There is an empty pot of coffee on your desk. And there is yet another blank sheet of paper in your typewriter.

You stare at the paper. It stares back at you. And nothing happens.

Any of these situations sound familiar? At one time or another, most people being asked to do some original thinking have faced the hellish taunts of a blank sheet of paper. This special torture is not the exclusive property of authors who complain of "writer's block." Instead, it should be called "idea block" because it affects the entire world of would-be creative thinkers. Anyone—novelist, artist, entrepreneur, designer, CEO, tinkerer-in-the-garage, middle manager, teacher, student, engineer, salesperson, farmer, office worker, housekeeper, assembly line worker, lover—can suffer from "idea block." It especially afflicts those who are consciously trying to be creative for the first time in years. To creative neophytes, a simple sheet of paper can seem to be an insurmountable obstacle. "I'm not creative," they whimper—and that blank sheet of paper is proof. "Why did I ever expect that *I* could think of a good idea?"

Fortunately, there is a path out of this barren ideascape.

There is a way to sneak up on that formidable sheet of flimsy white stuff and then ambush it with creative preparation and follow-through.

S.T.R.I.K.E.

These initials stand for six steps that will take you by the hand and show you how to have an idea—and then how to make that idea happen. The S.T.R.I.K.E. process is extraordinarily powerful. In its ultimate form, S.T.R.I.K.E. can launch industries, restyle governments, and thrill multitudes. But its proudest accomplishment is simply to bring that blank sheet of paper to its knees.

The "S" in S.T.R.I.K.E. stands for "Stew." It's how you begin, by thinking—stewing—almost aimlessly about all your problems, goals, and opportunities. What's not working? What's bugging you? What could work better? Is there something new you'd love to do? Give your mind free rein to mull over a thousand possibilities. Then, little by little, start to focus on some problem you'd like to solve ("Should I try to get a better job?"), some opportunity you'd like to explore ("Do I want to transfer to Portland?"), or some goal you'd like to achieve ("There has to be a better way to make that distribution system work.").

Now move on to the "T." It stands for "Target." From the rich grist that your stewing has produced, pick one specific objective and define it carefully. Be able to write that target down in *less than ten words*. Make it clear. Make it concise. Make sure it contains your goal. If you've been stewing about your job, there could be a dozen different objectives you want to achieve. Pick *one* of those objectives and state it in ten words or less.

The "R" is for "Research." Be adventurous in your explorations. Go to the library and get whatever books have been written on your target. Look at magazine articles. Write letters requesting information. Talk to people who know about your target. Ask friends to introduce you to their friends who might know about your target. Chat with bartenders, barbers, and taxi drivers. Take notes incessantly—and put together a file folder of scribbled notes, articles, reports, and relevant information that's at least *one inch thick*.

The "I" represents the fabulous world of "Ideas." With your ten-word target emblazoned in your mind and your one-inch-thick research file close at hand, you're ready to arm-wrestle that blank sheet of paper. First, think about the rules that convention expects you to follow. If you don't like them, change them. Now, unleash yourself. Be bold, spirited, and *visual*. Conjure up words, pictures, phrases, all the while keeping a close eye on your target objective. Be happy. Be wild. Be loose. Just be sure to write, sketch, or somehow record every little shred as you go along. Fill up sheets of paper with your scribbles and idea fragments. Then watch the incredible thing that happens. The best of your little creative blips will almost magically transform themselves into real, workable ideas. You will have a batch of ideas.

"K" is for the "Key" idea. In your bulging inventory of fresh ideas you probably now have several very good concepts. Force yourself to pick the *single best idea*, the one you believe will hit the bull's-eye of your target. Why just one? Because the most difficult part of the creative process is making an idea actually happen. If it is an ambitious idea (and I hope it is), accomplishing that idea will require *all* your resources. If you make the mistake of trying to push three ideas forward simultaneously, your energy will be splintered and you will dramatically increase your chances of failing on all three. Focus your efforts. Pick the Key idea. Then move on to the critical last step.

"E" is the undoing of most attempts at creative change in our lives. It stands for "Execute." Now you will be asked to leave the privacy of your office, your study, your garage workbench and take your fragile idea public. This is scary stuff because in order to make an idea happen, it often must be exposed to strangers—coldhearted, judgmental critics who will freely offer opinions of your fledgling concept ("Boy, what a lousy idea!"). Along the way, you may have to suffer many slings, arrows, and Bronx cheers, but it's vitally important to realize that *this is ultimately the most important part of the creative process*. You must be prepared to listen to the outside world, perhaps adjust your course, but continue to press forward. If you're selling your abilities or yourself, *somebody* has to buy or you're nowhere. Henry Ford and Thomas Edison were great salesmen as well as great inventors. So get behind your idea and push it. Make it happen step by step. When it finally does happen, give yourself a pat on the back. Then move on to invent your next idea, starting the S.T.R.I.K.E. process all over again.

Quite possibly, any creative venture ever launched and

accomplished can be roughly boiled down to S.T.R.I.K.E.
These six steps will unlock your latent creativity and allow
your right and left brains to work together in harmony, not
in conflict. At the outset of the creative process, the right
brain stews and stews about a problem until the left brain
says, "Enough already, let's pick a specific target." Then,
after the practical left brain has busily researched that target, the free-wheeling right brain thinks up a dozen different
ways to hit it. Finally, left and right join to select the key
concept. It's the one idea that can best hit your target—an
original, imaginative, innovative idea that will really work.
"Now we're really cooking," the left brain says. "Let's roll!"
says the right brain. And the right and left brains join forces
to make that idea happen. What begins as a tug-of-war ends
with the left and right brains pulling together in the same
direction—a truly remarkable accomplishment.

It can happen for you.

Chapter 6

A RECIPE FOR CHANGE

STEW, the initial "S" in S.T.R.I.K.E., is how every creative eruption begins to burble. It describes the hours, days, weeks, or even months you will spend mulling over the where-do-I-go-from-here questions in your job and your personal life. It is a time to be unsettled, undecided, letting good thoughts, bad thoughts, middle-of-the-road thoughts muddle around in your brain. To use that time constructively, turn over each thought and conjecture and examine them from all sides. Stay loose, relaxed, and ruminative. And try to avoid thinking of *ideas* or *solutions* to problems while you're still stewing. If any fabulous concepts occur to you, simply file them away for later consideration. Don't rush your stewing.

Stew about the "want" questions, the questions that whirl about your subconscious just below the threshold of awareness. As you allow these questions—all including the word "want"—to rise to the surface, they may sound something like this:

"Do I want to fulfill a dream?"
"Do I want to change my career?"
"Do I want to be happier?"
"Do I want something to work better?"
"Do I want to improve my job performance?"
"Do I want to please my family?"
"Do I want my family to please me?"
"Do I want to help the world?"

Stew about all the "wants" that surround you—but stay away from the "hows." "How" questions become too specific; they can be harshly autocratic in their demand for a solution. For example, "Do I want to be happier?" could be answered with a loosely constructed "Yes—somehow." But if you word the question differently—"*How* can I be happier?"—it suddenly shouts for a specific answer, perhaps prompting a too-quick, ill-considered response. Specific solutions come later in the S.T.R.I.K.E. process, so for now just stew. Take time for open-ended woolgathering.

What subjects should you stew about? Everything's fair game: your job, your aspirations, your avocation, your education, your lover, your spouse, your family, your friends, your obligations, your commitments, your hobbies, your sporting activities, the place you have chosen to live, what happens on weekends, what you like about vacations, what might be happening five years from now . . .

Stew . . .
Stew . . .
And *stew* some more.

Try to keep your stewing *visual*. As you have thoughts about your wants, scribble them down on a piece of paper. Make a list and look at it from time to time. Draw a Fingertoon of yourself with one of your "want" questions in the caption balloon. Better yet, print one of your wants in a caption balloon sketched on a photo of yourself. Then tape the photo to your bathroom mirror.

Sometimes, while stewing, it helps to get away from your everyday setting. It should be a place that makes no demands on you—somewhere you have nothing to do but think. Ideally, it's a place with an endless supply of rich visual stimulation. Some people can stew in their cars. But a possible problem is the attention you must give to the act of driving. (Or, if you're a passenger, the attention you must give to the driver.) I prefer something solitary where I can be by myself with no other person hanging around demanding to be talked to. For example, if I happen to be in Europe, I head for a train station. Give me a plush window seat on a fast passenger train and my stewing increases a hundredfold as the countryside passes by. I'll stare out the window as telephone poles, cows, and billboards flash by and feel my imagination sliding into the "free-flow" mode. You might try this by finding any peaceful place where there is an abundance of visual stimulation—it could be a park bench, a ferryboat, a big log next to a briskly running stream. Since the scenery is not telling you a logical, coherent, sequential story that demands to be listened to, your brain is wide awake, fully stimulated—but *fully available* to think about anything you gently nudge it toward. Take notes, doodle, draw pictures, and just think about some of the changes you'd like to make in your life.

At this point in the creative process, it's important to fill your mental pot with a roiling mass of wants, dreams, wishes, and fantasies. Then add a dash of problems, concerns, even a pinch of worries. As your mind processes this rich mother lode of ingredients, it will tend to move you in a particular direction, narrowing your focus. On your mind's horizon an objective—a target—will begin to emerge. Your target may be as simple as "I want to sell 20 percent more widgets this year" or as complex and demanding as the phrase belted out by a guitar-whanging country singer: "You can take this job and shove it!" (TRANSLATION: "I want to quit my job and find something quite different that is both more stimulating and more rewarding.") Once your stewing has announced its direction to you, you'll probably sense a creative tweak: the beginnings of the excitement of *change*. You don't have the specific idea yet—the "how"—but you've pretty much pinned down the neighborhood in which your soon-to-be-found idea lives.

So jump off the train, leave your park bench behind—it's time to head for home.

Chapter 7

YOUR TEN-WORD TARGET

Back during the dawn of the information era, the first computer users began to notice something fascinating. In order to tell one of those superlogical machines what to do, they had to come up with a clear statement of their problem —and their objective. The very act of reducing a fuzzy, loosely defined "problem" to a sharp, crisp "objective" would quite often point directly at a solution without even turning on the machine.

Albert Einstein observed the same phenomenon. In creative problem solving, he put great emphasis on precisely pinning down the problem to be attacked. In his words: "The formulation of a problem is far more often essential than its solution." With *clarity* and *simplicity* in mind, it's time to start "programming your computer." After you have stewed about a problem for a while, try to boil down whatever you want to accomplish to a single statement—a TARGET. It is the next step in the creative process, the "T" in S.T.R.I.K.E.

Let's say you're considering a career change. Your problem is that you're just plain bored with the job you've got now. After stewing about that, you finally decide you might like to find a more interesting position in the fashion industry, work in a bookstore, or raise free-range chickens. With that as your objective, you might be tempted to write your target statement as follows:

"I would like to find a wonderful job in fashion, books, or chickens that will allow me to take advantage of my fashion sense, my degree in English, or my love of the animal kingdom. The job should be exciting and fulfilling, have lots of room for advancement, pay me handsomely, and allow four weeks of vacation a year."

That, of course, is a ridiculous target. It is a three-headed monster—unfocused, wandering, and with unrealistic requirements appended to it. An objective must be succinct and single-minded. You may think you want to pursue those three very different goals, but you'll get far better results if you select a single objective. So narrow your choices down to one, then state your target in ten words or less.

"I want a good job in the fashion industry."

Make a Fingertoon of your target—or caption a photo of yourself—and pin it up. Think about your target each night before you go to bed. Stare at it each morning when you get up. Visualize yourself in the fashion industry. What are your qualifications? What can you contribute? What barriers might you encounter? Still excited about the challenge?

You have found your target.

Before we go any further, let's address the possible concern that you will need far more than ten words to provide a specific direction for idea-making. Any "communication consultant" worth his $200-an-hour billing rate could easily spend fifty hours generating a twenty- or thirty-page document of purpose and objectives that would carefully and specifically identify what should and should not be done. But ten words? Can targets really be effectively stated in ten words?

By 1980, the Ford Motor Company had gotten itself into a sorry state. Sales were down and Ford was losing market share at a rapid rate. Aiding and abetting this slide, the Ford car designs were mundane, constrained by a set of design rules that had evolved and accumulated in the company. For example, if you were working at the Ford Design Center back in the 1970s and were asked to design a new Thunderbird, you would have been commanded to obey a strict set of rules: (1) Design your car with an upright, bright grill . . . (2) Square up the rear of the "greenhouse" (i.e., design the rear window to chop down sharply to give that area a squared-off look) . . . (3) Include a phony bump on the trunk lid as the vestige of a nonexistent Continental spare tire . . . (4) Slap a lot of chrome all over the car. It was a strict list of "do this" and "don't do that" requirements that may have worked in the past, but were clearly not working now. Good rules had become bad rules. The company had no precise target.

In 1980, Donald E. Petersen took over as president of Ford. He didn't think the current Ford cars were particularly striking. So he ambled over to the Design Center and met with Ford's head of design, Jack Telnack, and a team of the top designers. As part of their walk through the studios, Telnack and his team showed their early designs for the 1983 Thunderbird. (In the automobile business, cars are designed three years into the future.) Petersen was not impressed. The new Thunderbird he saw was a "rather boxy thing" that adhered to the conventional rules. He asked if the Design Center could do better if the usual restraints were lifted. "Of course," replied Telnack. Then Petersen issued a powerful ten-word target to the Design Center team.

*"Design something you'd be proud
to park in your driveway."*

I visited Ford headquarters in Dearborn, Michigan, and
spent an hour with Donald Petersen in the morning, then
followed up with a talk with Jack Telnack in the afternoon.
I asked him a question. "Back in 1980, when Don Petersen
asked you to design something you'd be 'proud to park in
your driveway' did you know what you had to do?" Telnack
smiled. "That challenge," he said without hesitation, "was
clear as a bell."

The revised 1983 Thunderbird that was designed, with its
dramatic, soft-edged "aero look," was a rousing turnaround
success for Ford. And the car's look established a unique design philosophy that gave birth to the hugely successful line
of Taurus cars. In contrast, General Motors, still very much
hung up in its own complicated set of "design rules," took
several years to catch on and begin to imitate the soft-edged
Ford designs. No doubt it will soon be time to break the rules
again—and I'll put my money on Ford. But guess what?
When those "aero look" rules need to be swapped for whatever rules come next, *that same ten-word target* will still work
just fine. In the year 2050, whoever is CEO of Ford can say to
a young designer, "Design something you'd be proud to park
in your driveway" and—assuming there are still driveways
—this corporate artisan will go off and design something absolutely terrific.

You don't have to be a company president to put the
power of a ten-word target into action. Gael Greene is a journalist, a novelist, and a witty observer of the New York restaurant scene for *New York* magazine. She spends every lunch
and dinner hard at work sampling the best of the culinary
masterpieces Manhattan's most prominent chefs create—all,
of course, on an expense account. She knows people throughout the food world: the restaurant owners, the food suppliers,
the wine merchants, and the cookbook writers. She even
hobnobs with a few of her fellow critics in the restaurant-
reviewing business. This is not a bad life. Gael has actually

written of "the indulgent—indeed often decadent—luxury of a restaurant critic's existence."

Back in 1981, Gael awoke on a Sunday morning and began to read *The New York Times*. A headline caught her eye: MEALS-ON-WHEELS SCRIMPS TO FEED AGED. This human-interest piece told about a disabled 67-year-old woman who lived alone in Manhattan, confined to her third-floor walk-up, no longer able to go up and down the stairs. Roberta G. was one of 6,000 homebound elderly who received a single hot meal each weekday from a city-supervised program called "Meals on Wheels." Someone would bring a warm, nourishing meal right to her apartment. Roberta would always smile and say hello; often it was her only contact with another person that day. But, the article pointed out, there were no funds to deliver meals on weekends—or holidays.

Not on holidays? But Christmas was coming!

Gael was anguished as she looked at the photo of the woman in her tiny walk-up flat. She would be alone on Christmas Day—no visitor to wish her a happy holiday, to bring a gift of hot food. In contrast, Gael thought about the bounty of her own life. "How can we live and eat the way we do," she thought, "while our elderly homebound neighbors go hungry on weekends and holidays?" She knew she had to do something, and quickly she formulated a powerful ten-word target:

> *"We must share our abundance*
> *with our helpless homebound neighbors."*

Gael called dozens of friends in the food world that Sunday afternoon. She asked all of them how they could help in time for the coming holiday. It was a heartfelt appeal. By Monday morning, $30,000 had been raised—and Gael Greene had found her cause. In hundreds of walk-ups in New York that Christmas was not an empty one, yet the fund-raising had just begun. Gael, along with fellow food lover James Beard, orchestrated a series of small events and dinners that

raised money in dribs and drabs throughout the following
year.

When more and more members of the food industry
wanted to help, Gael began to search for a single grand event
to be the focus of her fund-raising efforts. Wolfgang Puck,
chef/owner of the Los Angeles restaurant Spago—inspired by
Gael's New York fund-raising efforts—had put together a
charity event for the Los Angeles meals-on-wheels group. He
had invited several chefs to come and prepare their speciali-
ties. In a sense, Puck had (Eureka!) invented a new kind of
benefit. Gael, along with Manhattan chefs Larry Forgione
and Jonathan Waxman, flew west to attend. The three New
Yorkers looked at what was happening and decided (Nibble-
Nibble) that the idea could be made larger and grander and
exported to the East.

Many months earlier, Gael's "target" had launched her
on a quest for a single powerful idea. There was no question
—this "chef-benefit" idea was it. She imagined a mammoth
charity event with tickets selling for several hundred dollars
apiece. She imagined New York's—and the country's—finest
restaurants setting up booths to dispense samples of the most
delectable dishes from their menus. She imagined that so-
cialites, celebrities, even Mayor Ed Koch might attend. Gael
returned to New York to present her vision with joy and
enthusiasm. The idea hit the ground running—and was met
with an overwhelming response. Restaurants clamored to be
included. Tickets were sold. And a tradition had begun.

Today, the annual "American Chefs' Tribute to James
Beard" (named in honor of the now-deceased James Beard)
is held outdoors at Rockefeller Center, where the ice skating
rink is located during the winter months. On the evening of
the benefit, any fortunate holder of a $350 ticket can walk
from booth to booth sampling fare from The Four Seasons,
Arcadia, The Gotham Bar & Grill, and The Sea Grill, along
with an additional fifteen or so of the city's—and the United
States'—best restaurants. Even though this is a New York
City charity event, the chefs who stand behind the flaming
grills include such notable visiting celebrity chefs as Paul

Prudhomme of K-Paul's in New Orleans, Mark Miller of Santa Fe's Coyote Café, and Alice Waters, who chefs at Chez Panisse in Berkeley, California.

Gael's culinary extravaganza has become a major event on the city's spring social calendar. But the bottom line? This one charity event now raises almost $500,000 in contributions each year—and every dollar goes directly toward buying and delivering hot meals to hundreds of elderly citizens. Keep in mind that Gael Greene is not a major corporation. She doesn't have hundreds of people, or dozens of people, or even one person at her beck and call. She is a solitary freelance working journalist. But she is also an enormously talented person with great compassion—motivated by a powerful ten-word target, to create an idea that worked.

Whatever your goal or objective, a simple, concise ten-word target will always be a great motivator. It will give you purpose, direction, and a supercharged push toward that one great idea that will accomplish your goal.

A SAMPLER OF TEN-WORD TARGETS

- Earn a bonus this year that's double last year's bonus.
- Find a new activity that will help me lose weight.
- Write a magazine article or short story and submit it.
- Think up and implement a new system at the office.
- Develop a new design concept for an energy-efficient home.
- Move to Texas and buy and run my own business.
- Do something to assist the staff at the local hospital.
- Get promoted to a position that requires more computer skills.
- Spend more time doing creative, stimulating things with my family.

Note that none of these ten-word targets is the actual *idea*. For example, the architect who decides he wants to design a new kind of energy-efficient house does not yet have the idea that will make the design work. He simply has a clear conception of what he hopes to accomplish. A target is a well-marked road map that points you toward creative ideas. As you move along that path, you will encounter a great number of ideas. But a crystal-clear target statement will keep you searching for the very best, most relevant idea —and help you avoid being seduced by ideas that are *off the path*.

So formulate your target clearly. Limit your statement to ten carefully-thought-out words. Visualize your target. Live with it. Fall in love with it. Get passionate about it. And allow it to point the way toward the next step in the S.T.R.I.K.E. process.

Chapter 8

YOUR ONE-INCH FILE

During the 1950s, Alex Osborn wrote frequently about the creative process. He has been described as "the father of brainstorming." In his book *Applied Imagination*, Osborn expressed the thought that a "well-filled mind is certainly essential to creativity." He refers to facts as "the wherewithal of ideas." So now that you have formulated your target, it is time to build your library of facts—the data base from which your innovation will lustily spring.

RESEARCH—the "R" in S.T.R.I.K.E.—is a matter of gathering all information pertinent to your target from all possible sources. The more facts you can pull together, the more productive your idea-making will be. Don't settle for the standard fare. If you work for a large company, the temptation is to call the research department and ask what reports are available on your subject. That's a fine place to start—but a lousy place to stop. Press on! Become an information detective and scout out information and facts from all conceivable sources: libraries, back issues of magazines, books—and best of all, the experts who already know a good deal about your subject. Your investigation should range far and wide. Your antennae must be tuned acutely. Like the frontier scout who can read volumes from a few wisps of smoke thirty miles away, you will be trying to glean both hard information ("Thar's smoke on the horizon.") and soft, inferential information ("The fire means they're stopping for the night."). Fortunately, you are not plunging blindly into the information wilderness. As you begin to experience the thrill of the hunt, there is a clear direction to follow, shining like a 10,000-watt beacon. It is your ten-word target. With it in mind, you *can* see both the forest and the trees.

Whenever I begin a new project, I get a fresh 9″ × 12″ manila file folder, label it, and start to fill it. By the end of my research efforts, I assume that folder is going to be at *least* one inch thick. It will be stuffed with letters, research reports, magazine articles, copies of pictures and book pages, and so on. I use a yellow marking pen to highlight the most important points so that when I go back through the file they will spring to my attention. Start the research process by pulling together as much written material as you can. Then go after the information bonanza you will find by *talking to people.* McKinsey, the high-profile management consulting firm, has refined the art of the face-to-face interview. When a company is "McKinseyized," a swarm of eager young consultants interviews people inside and outside the organization—from top to bottom—and compiles an enormous amount of written information. Only then does the firm move on to generating solutions. I suggest you emulate this process. The personal interview can be a rich source of information pertinent to your target. But casual conversation does not make for a successful interview. To get the information you're after, you should perfect and practice certain techniques—what I call "The Four Tools of the Successful Interview."

THE FOUR TOOLS

1. WIDE AWAKE BRAIN
2. LARGE EARS
3. SMALL MOUTH
4. ACTIVE HAND

As you prepare to interview an "expert"—and that's anyone who knows more than you do about your subject—keep in mind the four critical elements of a successful information-gathering expedition: (1) The Brain—it must be wide awake, prepared with a short list of intelligent questions, and fully focused on your ten-word target. (2) The Mouth—it must be employed sparingly; you have not arranged an interview with an expert to impress him with your own keen insights about his field. If you try that, most experts will be properly offended and quickly tune out. Employ your mouth only to ask specific questions and to say "Thank you" when you wrap up the session. (3) The Ears—they must be acutely attentive to everything that is said. Be especially wary if your expert begins to ramble. When that happens, open your mouth briefly and politely redirect the flow of information with a question that refers back to your target. (4) The Hand—it must be very, very active, writing down quick notes on all the pertinent points. These notes will be invaluable when you sit down later to reconstruct what was said. (CAUTION: you might be tempted to tape-record a key interview. If so, be sure also to take notes. Otherwise, you will have to relisten to the entire interview just to get the three or four most important points that were made. Tape recorders inspire intellectual laziness; a pad and pen require active participation in the interviewing session.)

A good rule of thumb: After a productive interview, your brain should be stimulated, your hand should be tired, your ears should have been in action more than 90 percent of the time, and your muffled mouth should have been engaged for less than 10 percent of the session.

Don't hesitate to pick up the phone if you can't get a face-to-face meeting. President George Bush uses the telephone intensively. When "researching" an issue, Bush is well known for making a number of quick calls to a wide variety of people. These compact, efficient conversations can be used to gather hard information and—perhaps even more important —to collect a respondent's unspoken, inferential feelings about the subject being discussed. Frequently, *how* something is said ranks right up there with *what* is said. Listen for the conviction in a voice; it sometimes tells you more than the words. Always take notes on your calls. When something is said with conviction, write it down—then underline it boldly.

Now, on to a most important principle of successful research:

SQUELCH ALL IDEAS

Just as it is important that you avoid "idea-making" in the "Stewing" phase, it's even more critical in the "Research" phase. While researching, keep your "idea machine" parked on the sidelines. You will discover that as you acquire more and more knowledge and information about your target, the beginnings of ideas will inevitably start to form. So why squelch these budding brainstorms? In a sense, your information gathering is analogous to the seeding of a farmer's field. You want to let all those "seeds" stay safely nestled in the ground. Allow them to slowly sprout as day by day they are nourished by sun, soil, and water. Declaring "I have THE IDEA!" is as if a farmer suddenly ripped a single three-inch seedling out by the roots—and then deserted his field and its thousands of other seedlings. A single premature idea can be insidious. Once declared, it takes on a power of its own. The problem (and it is much more of a problem for people who don't generate ideas on a regular basis) is that, at this early stage, you *fall in love* with an idea. The idea then shoves you out of the way and takes over; it will twist, bend, and shape the remainder of your research to support only its premise.

> **A too-soon idea can leave you with a half-inch research file and a half-baked concept.**

Whenever an idea starts to intrude, try mightily to slam it back down into your subconscious. Think of this as a sort of "coitus interruptus" of the mind. When you postpone the exquisite pleasure of idea generation, the deeper recesses of your brain will accelerate to an even more frenzied pace. Your gray matter will bubble and boil with the beginnings of a thousand ideas. Keep them locked up for now. Or, if you simply can't avoid having some ideas as you go along, note them quickly and put them away in your research file. Do not dwell on them, visualize them, or fantasize about them. Time for that later.

Here's an example of the research process. Let's say a young office worker named Donald wants to learn desktop publishing so he can use that graphically oriented computer skill to find a new job. Don stews about his career, then focuses in on a specific objective, stating his ten-word target in just eight words:

"Learn desktop publishing and get my dream job."

Where should Don start? By gathering as much written information on desktop publishing as he can find. This is the easy part; he will probably discover that an astounding amount has already been written about his subject. Desktop publishing is a prolific subcategory in the computer section of many large bookstores. Several of these books should be purchased, read, and underlined. Don should also go to the public library to see what books are available there and—in particular—check the magazine files. Recent articles may answer many basic questions. If the library doesn't maintain a file of computer trade magazines, Don can call the business offices of the most popular of these magazines and order a year's worth of back issues. He can also call computer trade associations and ask if they can send any recent studies or surveys that will give him more insight into desktop publishing.

At this point, Don is beginning to solicit informed sources. And one of these sources is the knowledgeable salesperson. The trick is to bag your quarry when the shop is dead empty. Don might try going to a computer store at 9 A.M. to corral a friendly salesperson. Sure, he'll have to fend off the sales pitch, but some careful questions can yield a bumper crop of information. Other informed sources: Don might visit a technical or art school offering desktop publishing courses and ask to spend a few minutes with an instructor. Who knows? At the conclusion of this research process he might circle back to take the school's night school offering. During all of this information gathering, Don is building his file bit by bit: articles, notes, copies of various documents, and so on. His file is starting to get satisfyingly thick.

Now, equipped with a basic knowledge of his subject, Don is ready to talk to experts working in the field. In what I call the "First Working Layer" of interview information, he should review all his personal contacts—people he knows who might know someone working in desktop publishing. Is there a friend, a relative, a coworker, a teacher, or a member of a church or community organization who might know someone happily employed in desktop publishing? It is almost guaranteed that if you ask twenty people for referrals, you will get an amazing number of helpful responses. Always ask your contact the pave-my-way question: "Would you mind calling Suzie to let her know I'll be calling?" If your contact makes that thirty-second phone call, your interview is assured.

When it comes time for the interview, Don should go in prepared to ask only three or four carefully-thought-out questions. For example: "How would you describe desktop publishing as a career?" "What's the best way to learn?" "Could you describe one of those jobs for me?" "Where can I get more information?" Finally, Don can move on to one of my favorite insight generators:

> **"What question have I neglected to ask you that would help me understand this subject better?"**

When researching, you should always go in to your first interview with a written list of questions. Add to your list as you learn more; refine your questions as you move on to other interviews. And always finish a meeting by asking, "Can you suggest someone else I should interview?" If your interviewee volunteers one or two new names, again ask the pave-my-way question: "Would you be willing to telephone and introduce me?" This is a tremendous way to build an information base. From a small initial group of contacts, you should be able to eventually reach dozens of informed sources.

It is critically important to take notes during an interview. I am continually amazed by people who seek out and ask an expert's advice on something—and then serenely nod at each salient point of information while a pad of paper sits untouched just eighteen inches away. No one I've ever met has perfect recall. You are going to be gathering a number of varied, often differing opinions that will tend to blur and blend together in your mind—but your notes will keep your thinking straight. There is an extra bonus to taking notes. It demonstrates to your "experts" that you think they're saying something *very important*. It makes them feel good about their own expertise and forces them to think much more carefully about their answers.

Most people have no idea of the huge amount of relevant information that can be gathered on this kind of hunt. One source usually leads to the next. The more you learn, the better your questions become as you roll along. Don't hesitate to call back one of your initial interviewees if you have a new question you'd like answered. And that's a lot easier to do if you remembered to send a brief thank-you note after your first visit.

No matter what your ten-word target, if you've followed this kind of information quest, your file should now be approaching that one-inch-thick goal. Review your file often, spinning back through your notes and underlined pages. Allow the file to give you an overview of your quest. You need to do this review regularly to help keep things in focus. With practice, an inch of notes can be reviewed in ten minutes or less. It will keep you on track and pointed toward your goal.

Now you're on the home stretch of your research. Begin to wrap it up by looking for "Second Working Layer" information—the sources you don't know personally or haven't been able to contact through a connection. It's time for cold calls. If you pursue this information politely, with brief requests for information, you may glean extra insights that will give your research file some additional oomph. Whom should Don call? Certainly he should contact companies that already employ desktop publishing artisans. First, he tries a company CEO's office with a single question. The secretary, of course, will not put him through to Mr. Big. Don doesn't really expect to make that connection; what he wants is to be referred to someone else in the company. If this happens, Don has power. "Hi, I was just speaking to Mr. Big's office and they suggested I call you . . ." Now when he asks his single question, he *will* get an answer.

Another tactic is for Don to call the public relations department and explain to whoever answers that he is researching the field of desktop publishing and understands that their firm is one of the leaders in using the newest software techniques. "Would you mind answering a couple of questions?" This is remarkably successful if you can catch PR people on a slow day. Typically, they are friendly and loquacious by nature—as well as open to answering questions and mailing any nonproprietary information they have in their files. Don might just luck out and get a package outlining how their company hires, utilizes, rewards, promotes, and feels about their desktop-publishing people.

This example of "researching your target" has been about desktop publishing. But the basic principles apply to any target objective. Looking for a new hobby? Thinking of moving to the East Coast? Want to start a new company? Just make sure your information gathering takes all these steps:

(1) Gather publicly available information.
(2) Talk to informed sources.
(3) Talk to "First Working Layer" experts you get to know.
(4) Make cold calls to "Second Working Layer" experts.
(5) Don't stop until your file is at least one inch thick.

Gathering research never really stops. It continues as you move on through the S.T.R.I.K.E. process. But once you've covered the five steps listed above, your file will be bulging and your intellect honed. You are *programmed*. Now it's time to unleash your brain and get creative. All those yammering voices in the back of your head are about to be heard. Ideas are yelping to get out.

The fun is about to start.

Chapter 9

HOW TO THINK UP IDEAS—
THE GUIDING PRINCIPLES

Ideas are not generated in a vacuum. They take a lot of stuff: facts, fancies, old ideas, odd musings—trillions of information bits whirling all around us. A fresh, original idea can occur when you put two or three of those bits together in a new way. Of course, if you get lucky, nature might do it for you (like the rockslide "arch"). Then, of course, you have to be perceptive enough to recognize the new connection revealed by the accident—and be able to make it happen again. But don't wait around hoping to stumble on a cosmic accident. Because the truly exciting part of creativity is when you go out *looking* for a new idea, pick out your own selection of those swirling bits of information, and then combine them in a brand-new fashion.

The "I" in S.T.R.I.K.E. stands for IDEAS. Once you start to focus on idea-making, you'll find that great concepts sometimes pop up when you least expect them. Or you may find that ideas are shy little puppies you must coax and cajole out of hiding. Of course, you've already put things into motion. You started the process by Stewing, which led to your Ten-Word Target. Then you journeyed on to collect your Research, and now you are prepared to generate IDEAS. So what do you do first?

SWITCHING ON

You must tell yourself: "I am now going to *think up ideas.*" For me, this is a mental set that requires specific switching on. I need to click into the creative mode. I do it with the simple act of reaching for a 14" × 17" pad of paper. For years, while reaching for that pad, I've felt my mind sliding into a sort of free-flow mode. I own a small advertising agency, and many of my duties are quite left-brain in nature: client meetings, marketing strategy discussions, research and media planning reviews, contract negotiations, billing questions, landlord relations, even the occasional legal dispute. You will rarely see my 14" × 17" pad emerge in those situations. I save that inspirational trigger for the times when my creative partner, Art Gilmore, and I sit down to tackle a new campaign or ad for a client. That pad of paper seems to say: "Okay, John, it's time to get cracking." It is like a seductive siren's song—and I have learned to obey its call.

What should your trigger be? It could be a big pad of paper. It might be a special pen, or the act of putting on old clothes. Or (particularly good for a lot of people) it could be enough just to change your environment. For example, move your desk to a new spot in your home and tell yourself that this is where you'll think up ideas. If you work in an office, pick an unused conference room or empty office and make it the place where you switch on. The point is that you need to send an unmistakable signal to your brain that the thrill of creativity is about to begin. Find the trigger that works for you. Then pour your right brain a strong cup of black coffee —and send your left brain out for a long walk.

Don't make the mistake of assuming that creativity is an activity you will practice only on weekends and holidays. Your "originality mode" should be available to be switched on twenty-four hours a day, seven days a week. There may be a "best time of day" for you—personally, I can really get cranked up at 6 A.M. (Erasmus, the sixteenth-century Dutch humanist, evidently agreed, saying, "The muses love the morning.") But no matter when you switch on, you'll discover that the more you practice thinking up new concepts, the better you'll be able to whistle up a batch of ideas on demand. Which brings us to the next point:

QUANTITY BREEDS QUALITY.

I have had this experience hundreds of times. A fertile idea-generation session has just begun and—voilà!—without even trumpeting its arrival, a terrific idea pops onto the scene. It looks great. It seems perfect. It speaks to me with a powerful voice that says, "You're done now. You've found the best idea." I always allow myself to fall a little bit in love with this new idea. But I also insist on being almost immediately unfaithful. "Let's pin it up on the wall," I'll say in creative sessions with my colleagues, "and see if we can top it." We push on and allow more ideas to flutter up from the subconscious. We ignore each new idea's wailings and importunings ("Hey, I'm a sensational idea. You can stop now!") and keep the pressure on for more ideas. Eventually, a funny thing happens. When we review our prolific batch of ideas a few days—or a few hours—after starting, those initial ideas never seem to make the final cut. We always *do* seem to top those first creative upstarts. It will be the same for you, so heed this warning well:

**NEVER STOP WITH THE FIRST GOOD IDEA;
THERE MAY BE A BETTER ONE
RIGHT BEHIND IT.**

Generating ideas is a wonderful, loose, free-associating process that allows your mind to churn through all the information you have stuffed into it. As your brain bounces happily along, your ten-word target will send out a clear homing signal that keeps you on course. I'd suggest that you print those ten words in big block letters on a piece of paper and tape it to a wall in front of you. It will be a powerful stimulus to your idea-making for, as the pragmatic American philosopher John Dewey said half a century ago, "A problem well stated is half solved." The rules and requirements implied by your ten-word target will help—not hinder—your creative output.

This approach to idea generation works for cartooning, script writing, solving engineering problems, inventing a new way to get a job done, concocting a new recipe, figuring out a new career for yourself, or just about anything that requires you to think up something that wasn't there before. When you're about to put things together in a new way "for the first time ever," you must set about it with eager determination. So activate your trigger, unhook the telephone or put on the answering machine, and start to freewheel with the bits of information you have accumulated. And—very, very important—follow this one magnificent rule:

**SKETCH YOUR THOUGHTS AS YOU GO
ALONG.**

Creativity is a very visual process. There is probably not a single creative idea that cannot be portrayed by a sketch of some sort along with a few descriptive words. Leonardo da Vinci's notebooks were full of drawings and written notations. A sketch forces you away from long, detailed word essays and lets you portray an idea in a looser, less restricted way. Your sketch helps to record a right-brain idea in a form that is quickly accessible to your left brain when you want to spin back through your inventory of new concepts. When generating ideas, I like to sketch pictures and scribble words, random thoughts, and concept fragments—the building blocks of new ideas. When a bona fide new idea appears I sketch its essence, then add to the scene a few "labeling" words. Remember, your pictures can be *very* crude—anything vaguely recognizable will suffice, from stick figures and diagrams to clipped-out magazine photos or Fingertoons.

Here is a case in point. Which of the following two "idea descriptions" is easier to grasp?

A. My idea for renovating the kitchen is to make the small window over the sink larger by removing it and installing a larger 4' × 3' window so that the bottom and left side of the new window align with the bottom and left side of the existing window. In other words, I want the new window to extend higher and over to the right more. I'd also like to install two short shelves, one on top of the other to the left of the new window. The wall phone should be installed to the right of the new window and the new dishwasher underneath the counter, to the right of the cupboard doors under the sink, and beneath the new wall phone.

—or—

B. My idea for renovating the kitchen is to do the following:

(1) Remove old window and install a new 4' × 3' window as indicated in the sketch.
(2) Install two short shelves as indicated.
(3) Install wall phone to right of new window as indicated.
(4) Install new dishwasher as indicated.

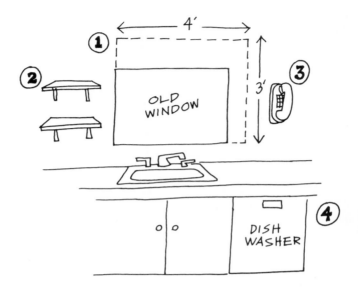

Here's further proof of the importance of the visual in conveying ideas. Thomas A. Edison was a prolific—and visual—genius. His papers are being published by a team of historians headed by Professor Reese Jenkins of Rutgers University. According to Jenkins, if the more than *four million* individual sheets of paper churned out by Edison and his squadrons of fellow workers, tinkerers, and idea-makers were stacked in one pile they would reach "higher than the World Trade Center towers." If you were to look through those papers, which helped to generate 1,093 U.S. patents, you would find that thousands of them carried Edison's explanatory little sketches along with the expected scientific language. Amazingly, in a letter he wrote in 1868, Edison stated: "I have for nearly 3 years been experimenting on a 'fac simile' which I intend to use for Transmitting Chinese Characters." Edison's sketch of a copying press demonstrates how his visual thinking easily portrayed a fax-like machine that could transmit characters over telegraph lines. If he were around to look at one of today's ubiquitous fax machines, Edison might smile a knowing smile and say, "Yeah, that's what I was driving at . . ."

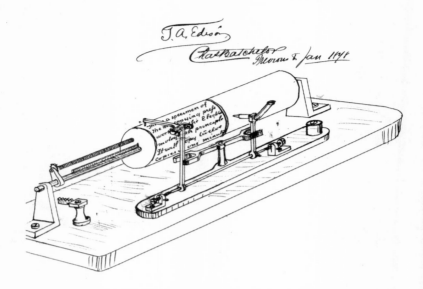

Thomas Edison's copying press sketched in 1877.

You can spin through a large collection of Edison's sketches-with-captions and in fifteen minutes get the drift of a hundred different things he was "driving at." You could never accomplish the same fast overview if you were required to look only at his words. This is one of the reasons you want to keep your idea generation *visual*. You want to be able to accomplish a quick review of your ideas many, many times during the process. This visual "parade in review" will stimulate new ideas, new combinations, new directions. It will give your right brain a chance to shine.

The visual stimulus can work in another way. As you generate ideas, if you find pictures or diagrams that are relevant to your target, pin them up on the wall in front of you. Add to them as new pictures become available. Mix your own idea sketches right in with them. Cook up a creative chowder and invite your eyes to the feast. One of the ways the Ford Design Center inspires new car designs is with something it calls "image boards." When setting out to, for example, design a midpriced car for young, upwardly mobile families,

Ford's designers put together a wall-size board of photographs and drawings. They use pictures to answer such questions as: What kinds of houses do these car buyers live in? What kind of watches do they wear? Where do they go on vacation? What kind of art do they hang on their walls? What do their coffeepots look like? How do they dress? As the swarm of pictures grows, an understanding of *who* is going to buy this car and *what* might appeal to them begins to emerge. As the design process moves along, the fresh new car designs that are created can be checked against the "information" the image board contains. Because it is visual, this checkoff can be done quickly and—again, because it is visual —the experience is not hidebound or restrictive.

GO A LITTLE BANANAS.

Ask anyone who thinks up ideas for a living and he or she will probably agree that *good ideas often evolve out of bad ideas.* Just like the creative "loosening-up" exercises in Chapter Two, off-kilter ideas can open you up to more creativity. Start an idea-generation session with a few practical ideas— but then loosen up and "go a little bananas." Force yourself to be a little silly. Push beyond the pale. Sketch and describe some dingbat ideas that could never, ever possibly work. Here's an exercise to get you into the spirit. Try to think up fifteen uncommon uses for a common straight pin. Start by listing five reasonable, practical uses, things like "a bulletin board pin," "a crevice cleaner," "an instrument to draw blood." Then, for the next five ideas, go a little bananas. Think of outlandish ideas like "a sword for an elf," "an antenna for the world's smallest radio station," or "an object to provide the Meaning of Life to a pincushion." After you've pushed your mind to silly extremes, return to thinking up practical ideas for your last five entries. You may find that these last thoughts are the best—solid ideas now equipped with a little sass and pizazz.

15 UNCOMMON USES FOR THE COMMON PIN

Practical:

(1) _____

(2) _____

(3) _____

(4) _____

(5) _____

Outlandish:

(6) _____

(7) _____

(8) _____

(9) _____

(10) _____

Practical:

(11) _____

(12) _____

(13) _____

(14) _____

(15) _____

Back in the 1920s, there was a creative man at Procter & Gamble named Vic Mills. Mills, a chemical engineer, was a fountain of new product ideas, many of which he got by looking at one product or system and applying its principles to another. One day he was thinking about soap when he really went "a little bananas." "I wonder what would happen," he must have mused, "if I ran liquid soap through an ice cream machine?" It probably occurred to him that the machine would add some air that would stay in the soap mixture as it hardened into a bar. He was excited to find out if this would give the soap better sudsing ability. So he got an ice cream machine and tried out his idea. The result, of course, went into the "Soap Maker's Hall of Fame." The new air-filled Ivory Soap did make better suds. But to the everlasting delight of small children the world over, it also *floated*.

So this is how you put your creativity into motion. Your information base is in place; your research file has been completed and you've reviewed all of your articles, books, and interview notes. Your ten-word target is posted on the wall in front of you. Flip your creativity switch to ON and feel yourself begin to climb out of all your tight, constraining little boxes. Grab your 14″ × 17″ pad and put all your thoughts down in visual form. Scribble notations. Push yourself to extremes—go a little bananas—and think about your problem in unexpected ways. Let the ideas flow; don't fall in love with the first pretty little idea that comes along. These are the general principles of idea-making. But that exciting process is just beginning. There are still some very *specific* techniques you can use to increase your flow of brainstorms.

Chapter 10

HOW TO THINK UP IDEAS—
THE NITTY-GRITTY

Once you get your ideas flowing, how do you *keep* them flowing? For one thing, you'll need to clear all negative thoughts out of your mind, and out of the room.

Kill the Critic

Dismiss the drill sergeants. Nix the nay-sayers. Suspend all critical judgments. Allow even the dumbest idea to surface and find its way to your pad of paper. Write it down or scribble a picture and keep going. Give even a bad idea the opportunity to flourish for a few moments. I once began working with a newly hired marketing executive who asked to sit in on one of our idea-generation sessions for an important new client. With his wire-rimmed glasses and neatly trimmed mustache he seemed a little uptight for a hang-loose creative session, but we allowed him a spot at the table anyway. Big mistake. Every time an idea was suggested that didn't precisely fit his conception of "where the solution lived," he would scowl and shake his head and mustache abruptly from side to side while muttering, "No! No! No! No! No!" Little budding ideas were snuffed out instantly. Windows of opportunity and exploration were slammed shut. The mood darkened and all creative spirit drained from the room. Finally we had to disinvite this wet blanket and, after the shell shock wore off, we were able to get our little creative engine back on track. Whether you're creating alone or in a group, stick to this advice during idea generation. No negative thoughts allowed. All ideas—even oddball ones—are welcome.

Be a Martian/Be a Child

This is another technique that works creative wonders. Most people approach problems with a static mind-set. Their first instinct is to ask "How is this problem usually solved?" and then they look at the problem as thousands have before them. Instead, try to think about the problem as if you were a newly arrived man from Mars. The Martian has no preconceived notions; he just observes and tries to make sense of what he sees before him. Take the story of the Martians who landed their flying saucer in a small town in America, studied the suburban hamlet carefully for a week, and then returned to Mars to make their report:

"Esteemed Commandant, we found Earthlings to be a very advanced race of four-wheeled metal monsters. These four-wheeled Earthlings live in small houses which have large structures attached to them where their 'service units' are accommodated. The 'service units' have hair and two legs and are built of soft, mushy stuff. They are obviously enslaved and do everything the four-wheeled Earthlings require. The two-leg units wash the Earthlings. They feed the Earthlings through hoses. And they

are forced to climb inside the Earthling any time it wants to go somewhere. It is our recommendation that we not attack Earth at this time as the Earthlings are a superior form of intelligence—with quite dominating personalities."

It is a slightly skewed version of life on this planet, but there can be an element of truth, the seed of a creative idea, in even the most offbeat observation.

Always throw away your preconceptions and look at your problem through fresh eyes. Have you ever seen a child examining an unfamiliar toy? She turns it over, shakes it, pushes it around, trying to figure out what it's supposed to do, how it works. Approach your problem with the curiosity and ingenuity of a child, as in another story reported years ago in *Reader's Digest*.

A large trailer truck has stopped before a recently constructed highway overpass. A group of adults is considering the problem: The truck trailer is half an inch too high to pass under the concrete bridge overpass and is tying up traffic for miles. There is no way to drive around the structure. And the only escape routes involve turning the rig around, backtracking at least fifty miles, then taking a much longer, circuitous route to the truck's destination. The adults on the scene are noisily advising the truck driver to back up and take the detour. Then a six-year-old wanders up and looks at the situation. "Why don't you let some air out of the tires?" he asks.

Like/Not Like

Martian and childlike approaches to a problem are essentially right-brain techniques. Now try a left-brain one. List every idea you can recall that is anything like the idea you hope to find. Has someone had to solve a problem that's similar to yours? What was his solution? And then ask of that solution: "What's like it?" Search for these preexisting gems. And don't limit yourself to your own field of interest. Loosen up and hunt broadly—often an idea from another area is enough "like it" to give you a creative tweak toward coming up with a solution for your own problem.

A recent story in *The Wall Street Journal* relates how, in 1967, inventor Joseph Engelberger was a guest on *The Tonight Show*. He showed Johnny Carson his new robot, a clever machine that could open a can of beer and lead the band. The audience loved it. And talent agents called to book the act on other shows. The Japanese, who were trying to develop robots for factories that would cut labor costs and build products more accurately, saw the show and had a very different reaction. Here was a "What's like it?" idea—and they wanted to know more. The Japanese government sent Mr. Engelberger a first-class ticket to Japan and invited him to address an audience of seven hundred industrialists. He fielded questions for six hours. The Japanese robot industry was able to learn, adapt (Nibble-Nibble), and ultimately leapfrog ahead. Americans saw that early robot as a novelty. The Japanese saw it as "something like" the creative solution they needed for their specific problem—and today they dominate the world market for industrial robots.

But don't give up on American ingenuity. Take, for example, Jill Barad. She's an energetic, dark-haired young woman who has become a key idea-maker in the toy business—an industry that lives and dies on new ideas. In 1988, Jill was an executive in product development at Mattel, Inc. The company has a long-running, hugely successful product —the Barbie doll line—and is always looking for new doll ideas. For several years, Jill had been trying to accomplish a specific ten-word target: *"Develop a doll that brings little girls and makeup together."* But she had yet to come up with the right idea. She had tried out a doll that came with little lipstick tubes and makeup containers. But when the doll was tested with little girls, it invariably ended up a gloppy mess. How could Jill somehow have a doll with makeup that didn't stain carpets and clothing?

Fortunately, right in the company, there was a "What's like it?" idea just waiting to be recognized. Another of Mattel's sizzlers was the Hot Wheels line of toy cars for little boys. And in 1988 they introduced Hot Wheels Color Racers. A kid got a yellow car that, if dipped into cold water, changed to ruby red. Warm water returned it to the original yellow. This chemical color change process worked with a wide variety of colors. Jill Barad thought about her ten-word target. What it boiled down to was that she needed a *nonmessy* way to get cosmetic colors onto a doll's face. Some "What's like it?" thinking convinced her the toy car idea should work just fine; if a car could adopt new colors, why not a doll?

Jill made the idea happen fast. In two weeks the company had a prototype of L'il Miss Makeup and were showing the doll at the annual industry toy fair. When the doll's face was touched with a cool water wand, the colors of light lipstick and rouge appeared. When very cold water was used in the wand, the lipstick was transformed into a darker shade, and eye makeup materialized. When warm water was used, all the colors disappeared from the doll's face. Within one year, L'il Miss Makeup was a fast-growing $40 million business. If it hadn't been for Jill Barad's pursuit of "What's like it?" thinking, this new profit center would never have existed. (P.S. Shortly after this success, Jill was promoted to president of the company's Girls and Activity Toys Division.)

Or you can ask the question "What's not like it?" Some time ago, a fire official must have been sitting around thinking about accidents fire trucks were having while speeding through intersections. This could have led to a ten-word target: *"How can we cut down the accident rate at intersections?"* The more expected solutions might range from louder sirens, to flashing headlights, to motorcycle escorts preceding the fire trucks, even to recorded Dalmatians barking from loudspeakers as intersections are approached. Looking for better ideas, the fire official might have thought about the basic run-of-the-mill fire truck and asked: "What's not like it?" And that could have led to this answer: A fire truck that *isn't red*. That insight (let's give it a "Eureka") quickly pointed the way to optical studies demonstrating that lime yellow is, in fact, significantly more visible than red. The creative solution was at hand. Since 1970, fire trucks painted lime yellow have been speeding more safely through intersections in a number of America's towns and cities. But tradition dies hard. A 1984 research study reported in *Firehouse* magazine pointed out that lime yellow fire trucks had been involved in *half as many* intersection accidents as traditional red rigs, yet today the color red still prevails in many communities.

Giantism/Tom Thumbism

To find a creative solution to a problem, sometimes all you need to do is take something and make it bigger. Several years ago, Magazine Publishers of America, the trade association for the country's eight hundred or so largest magazines, was looking for a way to get ad agency creative people more involved with the magazine medium. (Eschewing magazine assignments, copywriters and art directors usually prefer the more glamorous task of creating TV commercials.) So MPA concocted a creative awards contest with a $25,000 first prize for the best magazine ad campaign of the year. In advertising, there are many creative awards competitions—and this was the only one with a money prize. But it laid an egg. The association didn't put much promotional money behind publicizing the contest, and agency creative people barely knew it existed. In spite of the $25,000 prize, entries to the competition were minimal. "You know what?" one of the publishers said at a meeting. "Maybe we need an agency to promote this thing." So a number of ad agencies (mine included) were invited to submit proposals. The association had a relatively small advertising budget and the agencies were all asked how they would use it to promote the contest. Here's what we did: (1) We thought about the MPA's modest budget. (2) We dwelled upon the invisibility of the $25,000 prize. (3) We applied a little giantism. In our presentation, I suggested that MPA take $75,000 out of their advertising budget and add it to the prize. "Give your awards show a $100,000 grand prize, and I promise you that every creative person in the business will sit up and take notice." I gave a simple explanation: "$25,000 isn't magic. $100,000 is." Then I delivered the clincher: "And you won't have to spend much money advertising it. The prize itself will generate a ton of free publicity." The publishers on the selection committee were momentarily nonplussed. Then intrigued. And then enthusiastic. Our agency was appointed, and today the annual Kelly Award with its $100,000 prize has become an ad business institution. As you might expect, each year a flurry of high-profile publicity (all free) features the members of the winning creative team picking up their check. A big check.

Or go the other direction from giantism and apply some "Tom Thumb" thinking. Funny how Japan keeps popping up in creative examples, but a couple of decades ago somebody over there must have been sitting around at one of the huge electronics firms, pondering a problem. The company was building big, bulky cassette players the size of small briefcases. But it was also making palm-size transistor radios. Why not "Tom Thumb" the cassette player? That challenge no doubt started a headlong creative dash toward developing little, pocket-sized cassette players. The products that resulted, such as the Sony Walkman, are a "Tom Thumb" idea that founded a product category worth billions. So after you try your ideas out as *big* ideas, see what happens when you make them *small* ideas. And continue to put all of your thoughts down on paper.

Look/Don't Look/Look

You're a young Frenchwoman. And you're an executive vice president at American Express headquarters in Manhattan. To have quickly ascended to that position, you must have some unusual talents. Anne Busquet, a charming, straight-talking executive, did it by thinking creatively herself and inspiring her people (including the number-crunching "credit people") to feats of creative accomplishment. In 1986, she was given marketing responsibility for the launch of the company's first delayed-payment credit card. Up until then, the only credit cards American Express offered (green, gold, platinum) required payment in thirty days. The new card would be a critical, aggressive step and had to have the right name, design, and positioning in the marketplace. Hundreds of names were generated by dozens of people. Gradually, Anne and her team whittled the list down to four names: Centurion, Maxima, Complement, and Optima. Which name should they select? Naturally, the research department was hard at work with complex, sophisticated research techniques intended to guide this choice. But Anne reached for a little pad of Post-it notes and handwrote one name on each sheet. Then she stuck the four little notes, with their four little names, up on her boss's office wall—and left them there for days. Every time she walked in for a meeting, she and her boss would stop for a moment and look at the four little stickers. Visual input. Looking at four names simultaneously is a powerful screening device. Ultimately, three names were eliminated one by one and there was just one name left on the office wall: Optima. The program was launched, and today the Optima Card is promoted on television, in magazines, on store door stickers, and in millions of mailings. You see the name everywhere. But just a short time ago, you could see it only on a yellow scrap of paper—stuck to an office wall.

I can't overemphasize the importance of keeping every step of your idea-generation process—all those thoughts and glimmers—in an easily accessible *visual* form. Put your concepts up there where you can see them. Look at them. Scribble down all random thoughts that pop into your head. If a word or a phrase occurs to you, write it down. If a picture seems a more appropriate way to record an idea, draw a crude doodle to illustrate it. Look at all your visualizations as the ideas begin to proliferate. Do not criticize or edit your work. Let those idea fragments flow. If you have filled one sheet of paper, put it aside and begin another. Look at your visualizations. Move them around. Keep looking.

And then *don't look.* Put your sheets of paper away. Go do something else. Try to put the problem out of your mind temporarily. This seems to me to be a very important part of the creative process. It gives the left brain a chance to rest, but the right brain is still churning. You've certainly had the experience of trying very hard to remember a person's name and becoming extremely frustrated when you can't force it up from your subconscious. But as soon as you forget about trying to remember it and do something else—*pop!*—there's the name. So, for a while, walk away from your ten-word target and sheets of paper. Then come back and ambush them. Return to your target and papers and *look again.* You may find that new combinations and solutions fairly leap off the paper. When I'm trying to "break the code" on a knotty creative challenge, I look over my sheets of paper just before going to bed, thinking hard about the problem I want to solve. The mind is now in gear, and while your left brain sleeps your amazing right brain will keep working. Always keep a notepad by your bed to record those 3 A.M. thoughts that will occasionally jounce you wide awake.

I learned about the "Look/Don't Look/Look" technique during my first job in the advertising business, in the mailroom at Young & Rubicam's San Francisco office. Since my goal was to stop running the postage meter and start making ads, I began an aggressive campaign to persuade the creative director of the agency to give me a creative assignment. His name was Hanley Norins. A Groucho Marx look-alike, Hanley has a dark mustache and dark, darting eyes constantly seeking the next visual connection for a great idea. Hanley was (and still is) "The King of the Thirty-foot Pad." Whenever a new project started at the agency, Hanley would unroll a big roll of brown butcher's paper and pin the strip around two walls of his office. Three feet wide and thirty feet long, it would form a gigantic blank "pad of paper" waiting to be filled. As various copywriters and art directors shouted out random thoughts, Hanley would scribble them on the paper with his black felt-tip marker. The excitement would build as the paper filled with words, phrases, and explanatory little drawings. Members of the creative department would wander in throughout the day and add an idea or combine it with an idea already there. Walk in (Look) and walk out (Don't Look). Then, maybe a day later, walk in and ambush the paper again (Look).

The crossbreeding of ideas was thrilling to watch. A word

in the upper left-hand corner might suddenly combine with a scribble in the lower right. Throughout the process, Hanley was an enthusiastic commanding general—a high-spirited Patton stirring the brew as, day after day, new thoughts and concepts were added to his billboard. Suggest even a so-so idea, and Hanley would yell, "That's great!" and scribble it on his thirty-foot pad. Hundreds of ideas would be born, dozens would survive the initial scrutiny, and ultimately, one idea would emerge victorious.

During my first few weeks at the agency, I managed to scribble a couple of winning ideas on Hanley's wall. Just before my third-month anniversary, Hanley called me into his office and said with a grin, "Congratulations, John, you're now a junior copywriter." As the newest officially sanctioned "idea-maker" in the advertising industry, I bid farewell to the mailroom. But at every creative session since that day, I've never been without a big pad of paper and a felt-tip pen. The simple process of visualizing your ideas can stimulate new ones, show you ways to enhance existing ideas, and help you remember what you've done. Why does visualizing work so well? Maybe because—of all your sensory organs—your eyes have the most direct connection to your brain.

Have you ever seen a photograph of the studio Pablo Picasso had in Paris during the early 1900s? It was a wonderful visual conglomeration of furniture, paintings, books, fabrics, foods, jugs, jars, musical instruments, toys, and various assorted objects Picasso had found God knows where. The entire space was a cluttered churn of visual information. In a sense, the visualizations of the ideas you jot down on a piece of paper are your version of "Picasso's studio," a place where the mind is stimulated to take leaps, to look for new connections, to find new ways of putting things together. Always record your new ideas—as visually as possible—on paper. Stay loose and let the paper gain a life of its own. (Jazz great Charlie Parker once said: "Don't play the saxophone. Let it play you.") Record your thoughts with words and pictures. Then keep coming back to your sheets of paper with new scribbles and fresh insights. Put them away for a while. Then sneak up on your pages; jump them unexpectedly and look for sudden new connections. You are creating a visual environment—your own Picasso's studio—in which your ideas will flourish.

Be Alert for Hunches

The "Look/Don't Look/Look" technique is fertile ground for hunches. Sometimes a hunch will creep up softly from your right brain. On other occasions it will come barreling in with bells, whistles, and skyrockets. At first, you're never sure a hunch is a good idea; the logic usually escapes you (which is probably the definition of a hunch). But deep down inside, you *feel* it's a great idea. Your gut says, "Wow! This is a good one!" So I *always* give a hunch plenty of room to breathe. Suppressing my left brain's demand that the newly arrived hunch have some "logical" raison d'être, I simply record the gist of it on paper—as fast as possible. Once on paper, the hunch gains a certain concrete reality. Logic will follow in due time.

Let Your Right Brain Be Your Guide

Harold Simmons is a tall, rangy, seemingly easygoing Texan who is in the business of taking over companies. Not a love-'em-and-leave-'em sort of raider, Simmons prefers to stick around and make sure his new acquisition is run more profitably than it was by the previous administration. One other thing about Simmons: He's self-made, personally worth well over a billion dollars, and rather proud of it all.

Early on a Sunday morning, I met Simmons at his Dallas mansion. He answered the door himself in an open-collar shirt and jeans. We went into a living room that was the size of a small house and talked about creativity in the world of takeover financing. The ideas he generates are not product ideas; for example, a clever way to build a better mousetrap holds no appeal for Simmons. But ask him to think up a clever way to take over a controlling interest in the mouse-trap manufacturer's company, and he'll come up with a dozen or so brilliant ploys. "Most companies operate with too much capital," he says. If he noticed that the mousetrap maker was maintaining a huge backlog inventory of steel springs, and that the price of steel-spring wire was going up fast, he might buy enough stock to gain control of the company, sell off the unneeded steel wire—which is tying up capital funds—and use the proceeds to reward the stockholders with a big dividend. And get a load of this next twist: Since he is the largest stockholder in the company, his dividend might actually pay for his stock purchase. In effect, he uses the trap maker's own money to buy the trap maker.

I asked Simmons how he got ideas. "Well," he said, "it's important for me to get my mind off what I'm thinking about. I give my conscious mind an easy, routine task; then my subconscious can really wander around and pick up all these creative ideas."

"Can you give me an example?" I asked.

"I get a lot of ideas in my car driving to work," he replied. "I put on the radio. I sing. And then these ideas, they just come to me." Then he added with a smile, "Of course, I only work five minutes away from here. I guess if I had a longer drive—I'd probably have a lot more money."

Simmons is a perfect example of a creative thinker who lets his right brain be his guide. When you are in search of creative ideas, you will find they will spring forth anytime, anywhere. But ideas can be elusive things—like fireflies.

When we were little kids, we captured fireflies in a bottle. Think of your pad of paper as a bottle for capturing your ideas. Collect as many as you can find. Then you will be ready for the next step in the creative process.

Chapter 11

THE KEY IDEA

So now you have a collection of ideas—some lousy, some good, and some, you hope, positively brilliant in their conception and scope. Dozens of ideas, like a bag full of golf clubs. As you look toward that little flag in the distance that marks your target, you know you can use only one of them. But which club do you choose? That choice is perhaps the most important step in the creative process, the selection of your KEY IDEA—the "K" in S.T.R.I.K.E. Never be seduced by the temptation to nurture several of your brainstorms simultaneously. Remember, *it only takes one.*

"But," you say, "that's going to be tough; I've really got a bunch of super ideas here." That may be true, but one of them is always the *best* idea. How do you get to it? That, too, can be described as a process.

I've been flying small airplanes for over twenty years and along the way have taken a lot of training. All pilots learn to check out the airplane thoroughly before each flight. I won't start the engine until I've looked up close at the static air vents, the aileron bolts, the airspeed Pitot tube, the fuel level in the tanks, the landing gear mechanism, the engine oil level, the lights, the propellor, and a couple of dozen other things that all need careful scrutiny. Back when I first learned to fly, a wise old instructor gave me a piece of advice I've never forgotten. "Once you've completed your check of all those little things," he said, "walk twenty feet away and make a circle around your plane. Look at it as one whole unit." It has turned out that *stepping back for a good look* has allowed me to spot things like a tiedown rope still attached, a fuel drain left dripping after fuel sampling, and a loose radio antenna that I'd somehow missed in my up-close inspection.

Stepping back is sometimes the best way to see the forest once you've inspected all the trees individually. So let's step back from the idea-making process and take a look at it as a whole unit. Sticking with flying as our metaphor, I call this "The Idea Kite":

THE IDEA KITE

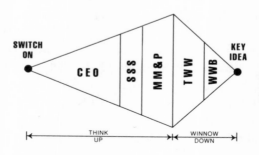

The Idea Kite is a visual representation of the way we think up ideas. Picture a kite turned on its side. The left-hand point is where you "Switch On." The right-hand point is your "Key Idea," the single best concept that you have decided to carry forward. The bigger, longer triangle on your left shows that you will spend most of your time generating a growing body of ideas. It starts with the "Churn 'Em Out" phase, is followed by the "Soak, Shower, or Snooze" phase, and moves on to the "Mix, Match, and Plus" phase. The widest part of the kite is the point where you have generated your largest number of ideas. The smaller triangle on the right represents the shorter time period during which you'll winnow down to the very best idea. This is the judgmental, highly critical "That Won't Work" phase, which is followed immediately by the "Which Works Best?" phase. Still "stepping back" to get an overview of the process, here's a more complete explanation.

1. SWITCH ON

Pull your trigger. Hit your switch. Head for your special "creative workplace," grab your big pad of paper, or just pull on your old jeans. No matter which switch (or all of them) you use, you are now telling your brain it's time to generate ideas. And remember, no negative thoughts are invited to this party.

2. THE C.E.O. PHASE

In the "Churn 'Em Out" phase, you let a bunch of ideas just pour out of your head—good ideas, bad ideas, so-so ideas. Permit them to flow, make a visual note of each one, and keep pushing forward. Don't stop with your first good idea. Keep churning them out. In a typical creative session, this productive idea-making may last from as little as thirty minutes to as long as four or five hours. But eventually your right-brain idea factory will reach a point of diminishing returns and yelp, "No more!"

3. THE S.S.S. PHASE

It's time to take a break, to enter the "Soak, Shower or Snooze" phase. Get away from your idea-making. Stop trying to think up fresh thoughts and head for a hot tub or your favorite couch. While you are relaxing, your right brain will swing back into action. Combinations you are not consciously aware of will be cooked up in the subterranean reaches of your mind. Back off and allow this little miracle to happen.

4. THE M.M.P. PHASE

Your mind is now equipped with a yeasty brew of those new insights and hunches. With a relaxed, rested brain, start with a quick visual review of all your idea sketches and scribbles. Now begin the "Mix, Match, and Plus" phase by seeing what new ideas can result by mixing two or more of your initial ideas together. Match up two wrongheaded ideas and you might find that a righteaded concept pops up in your face. Is there a new idea that can hook up with one of the old ones? How can you improve, or "plus," the ideas you already have? If the words "I wonder if . . ." start to occur to you, pounce on them. They're a sure sign that a hunch is coming down the pipeline.

5. THE T.W.W. PHASE

You've reached the widest point of the kite. Up to now, you've added ideas without particularly evaluating them. It is time to begin subtracting. (In the advertising business, this is usually when we invite the left-brainers into the room.) The "That Won't Work" phase is the period when the cold realities of life and the marketplace have their say. Begin to eliminate ideas that don't really accomplish your ten-word target. Eliminate fanciful ideas that cannot realistically be accomplished. Eliminate ideas you cannot feel passion for. The "That Won't Work" phase can be a difficult part of the process—particularly if you're in a group and must watch other people take potshots at your pet ideas. But this pruning of your idea orchard is absolutely necessary. You must reduce the number of contenders.

6. THE W.W.B. PHASE

With a handful of workable ideas remaining on the creative agenda, move on to the "Which Works Best?" phase. This is a time of positive thoughts and arguments. Become a champion of your favorite idea. Be sure to allow your emotions to play an important role in this selection. An idea that cannot inspire passion is a wimp idea. And wimp ideas are doomed to mediocrity.

7. THE KEY IDEA

As you try to identify the strongest contenders, the weaker ideas will fall by the wayside. At this stage of the process, you may still have three or four great ideas on your plate. But you must pick *one* concept—your "Key Idea." Why? Because the best way to succeed in making creative change is to pour all of your energy and enthusiasm into the accomplishment of *a single idea.* Anyone who tries to carry three important new ideas forward at the same time is likely to end up a three-time loser.

■

That's the idea-making process from a distance. You've examined it close up and stepped back to see it as a whole. The Idea Kite shows how you will generate a prolific batch of ideas, then cull them down to a single best idea. But how does the selection of a single idea work in practice? There are *five questions* you can ask about any idea while you are narrowing down your choice. Your tour guide to these five powerful questions will be Herbie Loman, the Vacuum Cleaner Salesman.

Herbie is stuck in a rut. He has been selling the "Super Belch-O-Vac" door to door for twenty years and has never varied his routine. He carries the machine up to the front door, rings the bell, smiles, and asks to be invited in. Then he dumps some coffee grounds from his briefcase on the living room carpet and quickly demonstrates how "Belch-O-Vac" power can suck every last granule out of the carpet's pile. Using this tried-and-true pitch, Herbie has managed to convince about six hundred housewives each year that they cannot do without the "Super Belch-O-Vac." At $50 commission per unit, Herbie makes a comfortable income of about $30,000. But last week his longtime supervisor was replaced by a young tiger, who came to Herbie and struck fear into his heart. "Herbie," he said, "sell twenty percent more machines or you're out of here."

Herbie went into a panic. He sweated. He strained. He stewed. And then he set out on the S.T.R.I.K.E. creative process, working with a vengeance. He'd done his stewing (S). And his boss had already handed him his ten-word target (T): *"Sell twenty percent more machines or you're out of here."* So he did his research (R) by reading every book on creative selling he could find. He talked to marketing geniuses and supersalesmen. He talked to bartenders, barbers, and Avon ladies. He even called radio talk shows to get more grist for his research file. Finally he had his "one-inch file" and was ready to generate ideas (I). He bought a 14" × 17" pad and began to scribble, doodle, and visually cook up a batch of ideas. Then he winnowed them down to the six ideas he thought were pretty good:

MY IDEAS
Created by Herbie Loman

- Hire an assistant to do the office paperwork while I make more calls.
- Convince Product Development to redesign the "Super Belch-O-Vac" in decorator colors.
- Persuade management to start a "Vacuum Your Way to Hawaii" contest—a free, all-expense-paid trip for the customer who wins the "sweep"stakes.
- Use cat hair and all-purpose flour instead of coffee grounds in my demonstrations.

- Produce a dramatic video to show on the customer's VCR. Demonstrate how the "Super Belch-O-Vac" can clean up filthy city streets, a junkyard, even a coal mine.
- Buy a funny hat and a fake mustache—then write a comic sales pitch that kids will want their moms to watch.

Which of these six ideas is the Key Idea (K)—the one idea that will best accomplish that 20 percent increase in sales? Herbie can find out by asking himself five questions about each idea and then grading each from 1 (not so hot) to 5 (fabulous). Then he just adds up the total score for each idea and lets the one with the biggest point total be the Key Idea. These same five questions will work to evaluate any creative idea under the sun—including your own brainstorms.

FIVE POWERFUL QUESTIONS TO EVALUATE IDEAS

(1) Does this idea hit the bull's-eye of my target?

1 2 3 4 5

(2) Is this idea simple in concept?

1 2 3 4 5

(3) Is this idea realistic? Can it be accomplished?

1 2 3 4 5

(4) Can I visualize myself making this idea happen?

1 2 3 4 5

(5) Do I feel passionate about this idea?

1 2 3 4 5

Herbie may total up his answers and find that—for him —the "funny hat" idea is a perfect 25. So he can move on to making his plan and putting it into action. And what about his other ideas? Once Herbie has worked out his new comic pitch routine—and made it work successfully a number of times—he might look again at his idea list and pick another concept to push forward. Perhaps the cat-hair-and-flour idea (Herbie rated it a "22") might be worked into his living room floor shows. But *always* get your Key Idea well launched before adding any others. Those five powerful questions will guide you unerringly to the best idea amid any prolific batch.

■

What about Herbie? Using his "funny hat" pitch, he increased his sales by 42 percent—and won the company's "Big Belch" award for superior salesmanship. The Key Idea concept worked for Herbie. And it will work for you.

Chapter 12

HOW TO GET THERE FROM HERE

Be strong. Get hold of yourself. You are about to set a course into frightening waters—because here comes the "E" in S.T.R.I.K.E., which stands for EXECUTION. Up until now in the creative process, you may have been working alone or with a trusted associate. This "tinkering in the basement" is very comfortable, cozy, and secure. But the next step requires guts, gumption, and a steely character. For it is time to take your brand-new idea and push it out into the world. Other people—cold, calculating strangers—will now have the chance to examine your idea and make pronouncements about it. And here's where most newly creative people make a fearful mistake. They somehow think, "This idea is *me*."

Their fledgling concept gets all mixed up with their own ego: "If you reject my idea, you reject me!"

In the advertising business, copywriters and art directors get paid handsomely to generate ideas by the dozens. Early in their careers, these admakers learn to separate their ideas from their egos. If an idea is "killed," they may be miffed at what they perceive to be a colleague's or a client's stupidity, but they do not reach for an overdose of aspirin. However, in the advertising business there are also some very smart people called account executives, who are more management-oriented and more left-brained and who do not usually generate the agency's creative fodder. In spite of this reality, once in a while an account executive will suggest a good idea, the creative director will applaud, and the agency will decide to go with it. So far, so good. The account executive goes home that night basking in an unfamiliar creative glow. But if at the next day's creative presentation, the client points out an undetected flaw and clobbers the idea, the account executive is usually devastated—flung into immediate depression. Why? Because as an infrequent creative contributor, he allowed the idea to *become him*. So separate your idea from your ego. You're here. It's over there. If your brainstorm gets shot down, there will be many, many more ideas to replace it. And, of course, there's only one you.

On the reverse side of that same coin, and equally involved with the ego, is the fear of failure, which can stop creativity dead in its tracks. I've worked in the past with Sir Peter Ustinov, the Academy Award–winning film star who is also a director, producer, symphony conductor, novelist, playwright, cartoonist, and notable historian who managed to write and publish a history of Russia in his spare time. Peter is a fountain of ideas—and he seems to make them all happen. I asked him once if this quality was hereditary. Was his father (a colorful character nicknamed "Klop" who flew for the Luftwaffe in World War I, switched sides to join British Intelligence during World War II, and was well known as a journalist) similarly able to make his creative ideas come to fruition? Peter paused, then recollected that his father had started a novel when Peter was a boy. The senior Ustinov had written several pages and then put them away in a desk drawer. As Peter was growing up, he often heard his father speak of the novel he "was writing." Except it never became more than about ten typewritten pages. *It never got out of the drawer.* When Peter himself was eighteen, he wrote his first play, then went on to produce it and cast himself in the starring role. Peter remembered his father's reaction. The senior Ustinov attended the play and then came up to his son after the performance. Father asked son, wide-eyed with wonder, "How did you *do* that?"

The moral of the story: Good ideas are too often left to wither and die on the vine rather than be offered up to a tough, highly critical world. Recognizing all that, you must now gather your resources, separate your ego from your idea, conquer your fears—and charge the barricades.

But before you set the world on fire, you need to focus on one important truth: *No idea has the power to get itself accomplished.* You've got to plot the course of its development. And the best way to do that is to outline your game plan on a single sheet of paper. List all the successive steps necessary to make your idea happen, and include dates for each step.

A PLAN OF EXECUTION

My TEN-WORD TARGET is: _____
_____

My KEY IDEA is: _____

The following are the steps I must take to execute my idea, and the date by which they should be accomplished:

	Date	**Steps**
(1)	_____	_____
(2)	_____	_____
(3)	_____	_____
(4)	_____	_____
(5)	_____	_____

To keep the pressure on, consider adding penalties for missing a deadline, especially if, like most of your fellow humans, you tend to procrastinate when it comes to accomplishing anything new.

For example, Brad Brazen has stewed enough to reach his ten-word target: *"I want to do something exciting in the creative arts."* His research turns up an eight-week night school course in close-up photography that he could take. He also finds out that a local community center is staging an arts-and-crafts show in six months. Brad starts to generate ideas. He comes up with a few of them, but nothing exciting happens until he crossbreeds the photo course and the art show. Suddenly he gets his key idea, and it scores big on "The Five Powerful Questions" of evaluation: Brad wants to exhibit his own close-up photos at that show.

Brad prepares to put his idea into action by outlining each successive step of his game plan. A plan can—and probably always should be—*very simple*. Brad's plan may change many times before the March 14 show. He may discover a second course he wants to take. He may experiment with video close-up photography as well as 35-mm still photography. The course may convince Brad that he needs $500 worth of equipment and he may have to alter his plan in order to allow time to buy it. He may discover another show that would better suit his work. There are many interrupters and alterers that may present themselves as a plan unfolds. But at first Brad's plan might look something like this:

___

MY PLAN
by Brad Brazen

Ten-Word Target:	"I want to do something exciting in the creative arts."
Key Idea:	"Learn close-up photography and exhibit my own work."
Execution:	Sept. 11 Begin eight-week photo course.
	Sept. 21 Buy equipment recommended by instructor.

Oct. 30	Complete course.
Dec. 15	Have at least 30 rolls of film shot and processed.
Jan. 15	Have at least 50 rolls of film shot and processed.
Jan. 19	Select my best 15 photos.
Jan. 20	Contact organizer of arts show and get exhibitor information.
Feb. 15	Submit selected photo prints and application to art show.
March 1	Keep shooting photos; try to beat the photos already submitted. If I can improve on them, substitute the better shots.
March 14	The show!

If Brad really executes his plan, pushes it along step by step, he will hit his target. And he will feel the excitement of thinking up a new idea—and making it happen.

How important is execution? Restaurant Associates is a company with $250 million in revenue, all from 130 restaurants located mostly on the East and West Coasts. Each one is a theme restaurant, which means that it's built around an idea. If the idea is "Tuscan-style Italian," the look, the feel, the menu, the marketing, and, of course, the name will all reflect that concept. Restaurant Associates has quaint French brasserie restaurants, spicy Mexican theme restaurants, "red meat" steak-house restaurants, luxury seafood restaurants, and was even called upon to invent an elegant, unobtrusive eatery to be located in the enormous lobby of Lincoln Center's Avery Fisher Hall. A very creative challenge: the concert hall managers mandated that there must not be a big, fully equipped kitchen and there must be absolutely no odors and no prominent signs.

The CEO of this idea-intensive company is a man named Max Pine. He's been with the company more than twenty years and became a major owner when a management group took Restaurant Associates private in 1988. According to

Pine, a man whose business thrives on ideas, "Ideas are worth zilch." People call him every week with "a great idea for a restaurant." In a burst of generosity, these callers are willing to share their gems if Max Pine will simply take the idea and make it work. Max always tells them this: "Use your own money—and you make your idea work. If it's a success after one year of operation, call me again." Pine, of course, doesn't really believe ideas are worth "zilch." But he does believe that the successful *execution* of a good idea is worth busting your creative britches for.

Speaking of creativity and execution, sometimes it is during the execution of an idea that the most creativity is required. For example, the top American at Sony USA is an executive who is both a physicist and a businessman. Mickey Schulhof, president of Sony USA, makes the decisions about which Sony products Americans will buy. Schulhof adds more zing to a nonstop schedule by piloting the company's three-engine Falcon 50 jet on his business trips. He holds all the necessary ratings and keeps himself current with frequent simulator training sessions. Back in the late seventies, Schulhof was called to Japan to learn about a great leap forward in recorded sound. In less than two days, he was briefed on the potential for digitally reproduced sound, the concept behind the compact disc. Early on, with no consumer research suggesting how the market might accept a totally new form of sound reproduction, Schulhof and the Japanese management decided to press ahead. Schulhof participated in the hundreds of little creative decisions that led to the development of the first compact disc player by 1981. So far Sony had gambled $80 million on both hardware and software development. Now the moment was at hand, the time to present this new technology to the ruling elite of the recording industry. Acceptance by the industry, and its willingness to junk its investment in equipment that recorded long-playing records, was critical.

In 1981, the industry's annual meeting was held in Athens, Greece. Schulhof had wangled a spot on the speaking agenda and was fully prepared to present the concept of digital audio. Taking the podium, he began (as a physicist) by spending almost an hour explaining the technology behind digital audio to the heads of every major recording company in the world. Then came the moment that (suddenly a salesman) he pushed a button and recording industry kingpins heard—for the first time—the superbly clear and undistorted musical sound produced by a compact disc. As a partner in the long creative process, Schulhof peered out at the large audience expectantly. Surely they would be stunned and amazed. What was the actual reaction? Absolutely *lukewarm*. Dismayed, he then began to understand the problem. The heads of record companies are all businesspeople—mostly lawyers. "It's an interesting idea," they said, "but our business is pretty good and we're making enough money and nobody cares if the sound quality gets better or not."

Fortunately, Mickey Schulhof is a very creative man. He didn't retreat, tail between legs, to work on other challenges. He went to the head of Sony in Japan and said, "This product is a winner, but the only way to convince the record industry will be to take a different route: *take it to the artists.*" He secured Sony's commitment and returned to the States to arrange demonstrations for pop artists like Stevie Wonder and Paul Simon. He told them, *"This* is how your music should sound . . ." Their reactions differed dramatically from that of the "roomful of lawyers" in Greece. Stevie Wonder, for example, was blown away. Three weeks after he first heard digital audio sound, Wonder ordered $100,000 worth of digital audio recording equipment for his studio—and decreed that from then on he would record only in the digital audio form. Other artists also responded enthusiastically to Schulhof's creative selling and began to badger their recording companies. The lawyers gulped. They swallowed hard on millions of dollars invested in LP technology. And they called to invite Schulhof to lunch.

Today, the compact disc industry represents at least

$20 billion in annual sales worldwide—and Sony has a big chunk of that market. It is a testimonial to creativity in execution.

■

Make a plan to execute your idea. Write it on a sheet of paper. Then get to work executing that plan. Be prepared to revise your plan with creative changes if you run into roadblocks. Remember that it's always okay to change your plan as you go along. (Just be sure you have a plan to change.) At this stage in the creative process, your disciplined, orderly left brain should be fully involved, so push yourself to make those dates. When executing your plan, you will be summoning up energy you didn't know you had. You've come a long way through the S.T.R.I.K.E. process—now see it through to the deliciously satisfying conclusion. Make that idea *happen*.

Chapter 13

ANOTHER LOOK AT S.T.R.I.K.E.

I first was asked this question when I was nineteen years old. A buddy came by my college dorm room, looked through a stack of over a hundred gag cartoons I had thought up, chuckled a few times, and then asked seriously, "What will you do when you run out of ideas?"

Since then, I've heard versions of that same question dozens and dozens of times. There seems to be a perception that every human brain begins life equipped with a set number of ideas. These questioners also believe that some people have a bigger idea inventory than others. (GOD: "Smith, here are your 15,386 ideas. Use them well. And you, Jones, I'm only giving you 16 ideas. You'd better learn to use a shovel.")

In fact, the more you practice thinking up new ideas, the better you get at it. If there is an unlimited amount of input (and there is), then there will be an unlimited number of ideas you can think up. And you don't have to be a "creative person" to dip into this honey pot. Follow the S.T.R.I.K.E. process and you will—repeat, you *will*—think up ideas.

One more key point: Keep it visual. As must be obvious by now, my personal theory of creativity is that it's a very *visual* process. So I surround myself with as much graphic material as possible. I try to create the visual equivalent of "Picasso's studio" whenever I'm preparing to generate ideas. It's why my office is always littered with pictures and notes taped to the walls, stacks of 14" × 17" pads leaning against my desk, and bowls of thick black marking pens at the ready.

I believe that true creativity most often occurs when the raw input data enters your right brain through your eyes, without too much interference from your superlogical, strictly verbal left brain. I submit that it is very difficult to come up with an *original* concept through the application of intellectual, logical, sequential, or verbal brainwork alone. For me, the eyes have it.

With that in mind, the following illustrations will take you on a visual journey through the S.T.R.I.K.E. process. You might want to use them as a kind of workbook, a quick spin-through of how you're going to create ideas—select the best one—and then make it happen.

STEW

*Woolgather, ponder,
mull, and muse
about your problems
and opportunities.*

TARGET

*State your target objective
in ten words or less:*

_____ _____ _____ _____ _____

_____ _____ _____ _____

RESEARCH

*Build a research file
at least one inch thick by reading,
collecting written information from all possible
sources, and interviewing the experts.*

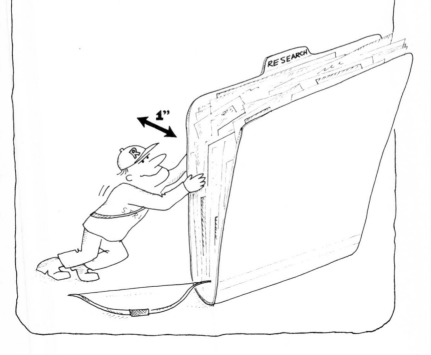

IDEAS

*Don't be critical. Switch on, and on any available
piece of paper, scribble words, sketch pictures,
scratch out scraps of sentences to visualize
your ideas.*

*Stay loose, have fun, transpose thoughts,
crossfeed concepts. Let your rich brew
of idea fragments steep.*

*Then put your visualizations away.
Later, return to them—and see them
with fresh eyes.*

*Mix and match. Add ideas. Subtract ideas.
Lo and behold, you will suddenly have*
   A WHOLE BUNCH OF IDEAS.

KEY IDEA

*Out of all the ideas you generated,
select the single* most powerful *concept,
the Key Idea
most likely to hit your target.*

EXECUTE

*You've got your idea, so now make a plan
and muster up your energy, enthusiasm,
salesmanship, and chutzpah.
The time has now come.*
GET BEHIND YOUR PLAN AND PUSH IT!

Chapter 14

S.T.R.I.K.E. IN ACTION

I have been actively using the S.T.R.I.K.E. creative process for many years. It has helped me generate hundreds—possibly even thousands—of ideas. Ideas for major ad campaigns. Ideas for building businesses. Ideas to enhance my personal life. But the most satisfying of those ideas was none of the above. It was an idea that defied the odds, an idea that illustrates the step-by-step success that can be achieved with S.T.R.I.K.E.

By 1969, I had been writing advertising copy at Young & Rubicam for eight years. When I was transferred from the San Francisco office to New York City, my assignments involved thinking up musical jingles for Jell-O along with con-

cocting television commercials for products as varied as
Vitalis, Tiparillo, Arrow shirts, and Eastern Airlines. One day
that spring, the entire creative department got an unusual
memo from the agency president. Every copywriter and art
director was being asked to submit ideas for a competition
Time magazine had just announced. In order to encourage ad
agency creative people to think more about the creative potential of print advertising, they were offering a *free page* in
the magazine to any agency that wanted to put together a
powerful, noncommercial message. You could "sell" anything that wasn't a product. The agency began to buzz, a
hundred writers and art directors all competing to do the
winning ad. As an ego-gratifying incentive, the members of
the winning creative team would get their names featured in
Time—the sublime seduction of "national publicity."

1. STEW

I sat down and began to fidget and fret around the edges
of this problem. This wasn't the normal, specific challenge of
an advertising assignment ("Do an ad that announces Good-
year's new, tougher synthetic rubber."). This was wide open.
The message could range from END OUR TAXES all the way to
PRAY FOR RAIN. But I was troubled by the thought that the
magazine page—worth well over $40,000—might not be ef-
fective. After all, this message would be only one page and it
would run only one time. We were to get just one chance to
grab America by the lapels. What a terrible waste if my idea
were picked and ran in the magazine, but amounted to only
a tiny whisper in the wind in support of some grandiose cru-
sade. I was not about to propose LET'S ALL PULL TOGETHER AND
DECLARE WORLD PEACE! Or the inspirational LOVE THY BROTHER.
Or even the worthy but impossible DON'T LITTER EVER AGAIN!
I resolved not to do a "That's nice" message—the kind of ad
that you look at in a magazine, murmur "That's nice" about,
then flip past to the next page.

Instead, I thought, why not use the page to make something valuable happen? Why not pick a small, manageable
objective that a one-time message in a national magazine

might really accomplish? My stewing had just come to an end. I had my ten-word target:

2. TARGET

> "Create an ad that will actually
> make something good happen."

3. RESEARCH

I started my research by looking at several collections of award-winning ads to see what kinds of public service ads had been done in the past. There were some great, highly creative ads for a number of high-minded causes. For example, one series of ads had helped recruit volunteers for the Peace Corps—but those ads were part of a long-running public service campaign and each had run a number of times in a wide variety of publications. I went to the library and pulled articles about charity drives and worthy causes. I sought out the advice of a friend who worked for the City of New York. "Is there something small the city needs?" I asked. We talked about bridges that needed repair, subways that were dirty and slow, and schools that needed more teachers. We also talked about New York's kids. I made notes. Lots of notes. My one-inch file was soon at least two inches thick. But this assignment had a deadline and it was fast approaching. It was time to generate ideas.

4. IDEAS

Alone in my office, I reviewed my notes, pulled out a big pad of paper, and told myself (as I always have), "It's time to think up ideas." I scribbled down every idealistic, hare-brained idea as it occurred to me. I put my sheets of paper away and came back to them every two or three hours. I added ideas, crossed out ideas, combined ideas. I had breakfast, lunch, and dinner with the assignment and pinned the most promising idea scribbles to my office wall, looking at them off and on throughout the day. I continued to generate ideas, sleeping on the assignment for three nights and waking up regularly at 3 A.M. to jot down more ideas. All in all, my idea sketches numbered over thirty. But throughout this whole process, I kept coming back to ideas that could help kids—city kids—ghetto kids who didn't have the advantages I'd had growing up in the gentle serenity of southern Michigan. Could the ad create ball fields for kids? A lovely country camp for city kids? A special educational program for the schools? Whatever the idea, I kept telling myself, it had to be simple in scope, or it might fail due to its complexity. Was there one small idea, a simple idea, that could actually be *accomplished* thanks to this single exposure in a national magazine? As I shuffled through my scribbles again and again, one idea began to push its way to the surface. This was a magical moment for me. This was just exactly the way the creative process is supposed to work.

5. KEY IDEA

"Maybe what I'm trying to say is . . .

"What if it was . . .

"Or . . . wait a minute. Why not this message?"

An ad seeking donations to build a small park in Harlem.

■

That was it. I pulled out a new piece of paper and within seconds the key idea became a headline: "How you can build a small park in Harlem." A site could be chosen, and a photograph would show a vacant, rubble-strewn city lot sandwiched between two tenement buildings. The ad would ask for donations from all over the United States to construct a tiny little park in one neighborhood in Harlem. It wouldn't take an awful lot of money—and the ad would probably bring in the necessary funds. I was getting excited. Suddenly I believed absolutely that this idea would be chosen out of the huge batch of ads being developed by other creative people at Y&R. I could envision my ad running in *Time*, then collecting dollars and checks. Most of all, I believed a park would be built. There was simply not a question in my mind. *I believed!*

6. EXECUTE

After that things began to move quickly. A committee of top agency executives selected my ad as the winner from among the hundred or so ideas submitted. Authorized to gather a park ad squad, I recruited a talented art director named Gerry Severson and a "crash-through-walls-to-get-it-done" detail man named Remar Sutton. We surveyed all of New York City's ghetto neighborhoods and began to talk with block associations. We settled on 115th Street in Harlem, a block with a strong neighborhood group that was eager to work with us. The community group suggested an ideal spot for a small park—a junk-heaped, deserted lot owned by the city.

The next few days were a jumble of meetings with agency executives, New York City officials, contractors, and equipment suppliers. The project could have aborted at any time. But I had the unswerving belief of a tub-thumping evangelist. We got city permission to use the vacant lot and photographed "one-twelfth of an acre of broken glass, trash, and rats." We produced the ad, sent the materials to *Time*, and held our breath. The ad appeared in the October 20, 1969, issue.

Then—and only then—did I begin to wonder if the idea would really *work*. But my confidence came surging back in the form of huge, bulging sacks of mail. Day after day the letters and contributions poured in. Our appeal collected nickels from schoolkids and dollars from all over the world. One kid wrote, "I like to play in the park. Please use the enclosed (a nickel) to build a park for another little boy. [signed] Bob, age 5." A one-dollar bill came clipped to a note, "Please plant a tree." And a great letter from a Navy man: "Dear Sirs: I didn't have any cash on hand so I bet a buddy of mine I could do one thousand situps. So here's his five dollars. I could and did!"

This one-time ad continued to bring in donations for

The "park ad" as it appeared in *TIME* magazine.

more than four months. We collected over $45,000, enough to build a far better park than we had thought possible. An enthusiastic adman—turned—landscape architect named Bill Hawkey came up with an innovative design to get the most out of our tiny space. Local Harlem contractors bulldozed the lot, poured concrete foundations, and built brick walls along the sides and back. Neighbors pitched in to construct a play area in front with high-tech climbing bars and a big sand pit for the kids. At the rear of the park there was a quiet area with grass, trees, and benches for the older residents of the neighborhood. The park even had a name. The kids were all crazy about a Chihuahua named Kenny; he sort of belonged to every child on the block. But the week before the park's dedication, Kenny scampered into the street and was hit by a car. The children dug a tiny grave under a young oak sapling. And began to call the park Kenny's Park.

■

If you want to generate a truly creative idea, start by stewing. Select a ten-word target. Accumulate at least an inch of research. Engage in a visual frenzy of idea-making. Pick the key idea. Make a plan and execute it with enthusiasm. The result will almost always be a creative change that makes something exciting happen. I've been doing it this way for most of my life. And S.T.R.I.K.E. hasn't failed me yet.

PART III

Rocket Fuel: How to Make Your Ideas Happen

Chapter 15

THE WORLD'S MOST VITAL SKILL

One evening I attended a cocktail party with a fashionable group of Manhattanites who represented all of the "hot" professions. Lawyers were gabbing with investment bankers, stockbrokers were comparing notes with chief financial officers, art dealers were chatting with magazine editors. And, of course, there were a few television and movie people in the brew. I was standing with the Senior Vice President of Marketing of a major packaged goods company. Suddenly up walked a crisply tailored, attractive young woman whose very demeanor screamed "MBA." She introduced herself and, without pausing for breath, imparted the information that she was a brand manager for a large, aggressive cosmetics company. At that point, she smiled sweetly at the marketing director and asked, "What do you do?"

He smiled back. "I'm a salesman," he said.

Truer words were never spoken. Unfortunately, those homely words instantly drove our MBA into the waiting arms of a Wall Street banker. But, in fact, we are all salesmen and saleswomen. Any time you want to influence another human being to aid, abet, or approve your course of action, you are *selling*. If you want to get a better position in another department at work, you'll have to sell. If you want your wife to agree to a scuba-diving vacation in St. Croix (and she's a Colorado-bound backpacker), you'll have to sell. If you want to buy a used car for 10 percent less than the seller is asking, then you—and not the seller—will be doing the selling. Build a better mousetrap and the world will not beat a path to your doorstep. The world will yawn and the mice will chuckle. But aggressively *sell* your mousetrap to investors or to a company that markets such contraptions, and the world *will* beat that path to your doorstep. Only now your doorstep will be attached to a considerably larger house on the highest hill in town.

Salesmanship is an essential ingredient in making your ideas happen. And despite the conventional wisdom, selling can—and should—be a very creative and challenging process. Anyone who tells you otherwise should look at the career of Peter Diamandis. Peter is a big (he was a heavyweight boxer in college), brash Greek who spent more than three decades as an employee of other people. By 1987 he had clambered up the hierarchy at the CBS Magazine Group and was a well-paid executive working to make magazines more important in a television-oriented company. In fact, two years earlier, Peter had masterminded the group's acquisition of twelve consumer magazines from Ziff-Davis, titles like *Skiing*, *Flying*, and so on, for the tidy sum of $362.5 million. But in 1987, Larry Tisch showed up as the new owner running CBS, and to reduce the company's debt he started to unload some assets. The first to go was book publisher Holt, Rinehart and Winston. Next, Tisch got an unsolicited offer from Hachette, the largest publisher and broadcaster in France: $600 million for those magazines Diamandis had paid less than $400 million for. Tisch was interested in selling, but Diamandis asked for a little time to see if he could put together his own leveraged buyout offer. Mind you, Peter Diamandis was not independently wealthy—he was paying a mortgage and educating a flock of kids. "Okay, Peter, see what you can do," said Tisch. "You can have a month."

How exactly do mortgage-paying citizens go about raising in excess of $600 million? Peter wasn't sure, but he tried some Wall Street resources. No deal. Then a friend suggested that Peter contact someone at the Prudential Insurance Company. He did. Which led to a brief meeting with one corporate youngster. Peter did an hour of "Magazines 101" and left. The next day he was asked to come again and this time met with two corporate kids. He did a rerun of "Magazines 101" and left. A few days later, they called and asked for some financial information, which Peter provided. A week later, Peter was asked if he could attend a meeting of the Prudential board of directors in Newark, New Jersey. "Why not?" he thought.

That day, Peter walked into the largest meeting room he'd ever seen. About forty men wearing blue suits and white shirts sat around a huge table. No smiles. No introductions. Fortunately, Peter is not shy. Summoning up years of sales experience, he strode to the center of the room and introduced himself. Peter knew that the Pru had never before totally backed an LBO; he was surrounded by an awful lot of suspicious faces. Nevertheless, he launched into his presentation with enthusiasm and for one straight hour held the group's rapt attention. He proclaimed the glories of the magazine industry. He spun images of profitability. He sold hard on the inherent value of the CBS magazines. But the thing Peter probably sold hardest—was himself.

Those forty white shirts bought Peter's pitch. The result was a check for $650 million and an agreement that gave Diamandis a significant share of any growth. Larry Tisch spurned the lower Hachette offer and made the deal at $650 million with Diamandis, who became CEO of the newly formed LBO. In an act of characteristic unbashfulness, Peter renamed the company Diamandis Communications.

Follow these next numbers carefully: Peter immediately sold off some of the magazines for about $300 million, reducing Prudential's investment to $350 million. Then only eight months after buying the company, Peter went back to the previous suitor, Hachette, and sold the *remaining* titles to them for *$712 million*. (I told you he was a salesman.) On this less-than-a-year flip, Diamandis and Prudential made more than a $350 million profit. Peter had set up his key executives so that twenty of them became instant millionaires. And Peter himself took home a paycheck rumored to be somewhat north of $30 million.

Is selling a God-given ability that is sparsely sprinkled throughout the world? Or can it be learned? Fortunately, the principles of selling are well known. The bookstores are filled with "how to sell" books, and there are classes you can take to learn this invaluable skill. Back in the late sixties, one of my best friends was an advertising-guy-turned-television-comedy-writer named Steve Gordon. Steve was the funniest, most brilliant creative guy I'd ever met. Get him alone with a few intimate friends, and he would sparkle with wacko one-liners. But Steve had a problem, one that I shared. Neither one of us could sell worth a damn. Put us into a conference room and we would just sort of choke up. We were both concerned that this lack of salesmanship was hindering the upward surge of our careers.

"Let's take the Dale Carnegie Course," I suggested.

"That's for shoe salesmen," Steve said.

"It'll cost us about five hundred dollars," I persisted.

"It's for expensive shoe salesmen," Steve countered.

I prevailed, and we signed up for the fourteen-week course. Our classmates were an odd bunch, about thirty people ranging from Westchester housewives and tongue-tied accountants to a Cuban Bay of Pigs veteran. All in all, we were a crew of shakers, shudderers, and stammerers. Each week we had to make a speech. We were never allowed to read from notes; everything had to come from your head. Gradually one of the big secrets of salesmanship began to sink in: Always speak about (and always "sell") something you know from your own experience.

Then came a breakthrough session. Our regular instructor didn't show up, and his substitute that night was a short, bald, meek-looking man. He shuffled to the front of the class and introduced himself in a low mumble while staring at his shoes. He stumbled and fumbled. And—as a class—we began to squirm uncomfortably. "Good heavens!" we all thought. "Who *is* this total incompetent?" He then took a section of newspaper and began to roll it up nervously. This pitiful wimp had clearly lost his way.

"Ka-WHAM!" The newspaper bat exploded on the rostrum.

"We!" the man suddenly bellowed out. "Are going to talk about *salesmanship!* I have just given you a demonstration of the worst (a bang of the newspaper bat to emphasize the point) possible (another bang) way to stand up in front of (BAM!) a group of people! If you don't believe (BAM!) passionately and (BAM!) enthusiastically in what you're saying, then how in the world do you ever expect to sell your point (BAM!) to an important (BAM!) audience (BAM!)?"

The class was stunned. Wimp had become Superman before our very eyes. And the only thing that had changed was his energy and enthusiasm. The man was spectacular. During that watershed session, we took turns at rolling up newspaper bats and walloping away at the table as we roared out our speeches. The course taught us to stand up and think on our feet. It taught us never to read from a script. It taught us techniques to hold the attention of an audience. Most of all, it taught us to sell from our guts. At the conclusion of the course, Steve and I had achieved something that, just fourteen weeks before, had seemed ridiculously unobtainable. We now had the ability to stride into the den of a wary client and —with an irresistible belief in ourselves and our work—*sell the idea we wanted to sell.*

Several years later, Steve began to branch out from the

world of situation comedies. After finishing his TV scripts each day, he'd work on his idea for a movie: the story of a very wealthy drunk and his addled life. He completed the script and began to peddle it around town. Then he got his big break: A major studio bought his idea for a movie called *Arthur*. They all agreed that Dudley Moore would be great in the lead role, Liza Minnelli would excel as Arthur's girlfriend, and Sir John Gielgud would make a superb manservant to the very rich, very drunk master of the house.

Next the studio executives began to think about who the director should be for this wonderfully funny script. "I'd like to direct it myself," Steve said. The execs were flabbergasted. "But you've never directed anything," they protested. "And this film will have a production budget of ten million dollars." After very little discussion they made their decision: "Sorry, Steve, but we can't afford to blow it."

Steve might have stopped there. After all, he'd sold his first major movie script. This was the big time, and these slick Hollywood guys were surely experts on how to make a movie. But he didn't stop. Instead he began to *sell*. With humor, confidence, conviction, and fervor he chipped away at the studio's resistance. Sure, he was a little-known "TV writer." Sure, he'd never directed anything. But the guy apparently was "a born salesman" and he did have that crazy sense of humor that kept surfacing through all the negotiations. Steve persisted. And persisted. Finally they gave in with an exasperated "Okay, Steve, you've got it." In his debut as a director, Steve rewrote *Arthur* each day on the set as new gags jumped into his head. The film, of course, benefited from these day-to-day rewrites and became a comedy classic. And Steve's ability to sell—an ability that can be learned—contributed immensely to the final result.

Unfortunately, two years later, Steve Gordon was stricken with a heart attack and died at the age of forty-five. A truly funny man was gone, and the world had lost the ten or even twenty great films that were locked up in his brain. But wherever Steve is—somewhere out there—I'm sure he's *selling* a very funny idea to someone.

■

You, too, can learn to sell. It is a skill that will serve you extraordinarily well in moving your ideas ahead. Whether you are a surgeon or a cop on the beat, a housewife or a corporation biggie, the ability to convince other people will bring great benefits to you. It works this way. First, your "ability to sell" shows them why your idea is a good one. Second, it shows them that you have the internal fire necessary to push your idea to a successful conclusion.

People like to back a winner. And being a winner is what selling is all about.

Chapter 16

RAH!

We will now deal with the most exciting force in the world of ideas. It is the high-octane juice that will get you off your duff and make your ideas really happen. What is this magic stuff? It is the miracle of:

ENTHUSIASM

Without this extra boost, your brilliant idea may languish. It might just—in the colorful language of a Catskills comedian—"lie there like a latka." But rather than listen to comedians, let's call on some real experts. Ralph Waldo Emerson said, *"Nothing great was ever achieved without enthusiasm."* Albert Einstein, one of the keenest minds of all time, said, *"Enthusiasm is more important than intelligence."* And Georg Wilhelm Friedrich Hegel left no room for doubt: *"Of this I am certain. Absolutely nothing great in this world has been accomplished without passion."*

Making a unique, creative idea happen might possibly be a new experience for you. If so, naturally, you'll have doubts. You'll have second thoughts. You'll wonder if you can really make this marvelous concept happen. And if the successful realization of your idea requires the participation of other people, you may be doubled over with apprehension. If all of these terrible reservations are afflicting you, what should you do?

Try enthusiasm. Become a cheerleader for your idea. Fall in love with your concept and convince yourself that it far exceeds the invention of sliced bread or the steam engine. You don't have to whack the table with a newspaper or come out with a steady stream of one-liners. Enthusiasm comes in many styles, from quiet persistence to vigorous drum beating. And it all stems from the same source: a deep belief in the value of your idea. Sometimes an idea is so good that it speaks for itself. But far more often, *you* are the spokesperson and you must muster up the necessary passion. Where will you find it? Once you truly *believe* in an idea, enthusiasm will follow almost naturally.

Since advertising is an "idea-making business," I have come up with a few creative concepts in my day. Because I believed in them, enthusiasm inevitably became part of my pitch. When I presented my ideas, explained them, and then ultimately sold them to clients who would put up the millions of hard dollars required to go public with a major ad campaign, it was my passionate conviction that helped win the day. These, of course, were fairly big-time decisions. Big, expensive ideas. However, one of my most satisfying ideas was a modest one that I cooked up (pun intended) in the nonbusiness realm—my invention of the "Bachelor Cooking Class."

Back in the late seventies, my ten-year marriage fell apart, a divorce brought on by the pressures of two careers

bumping into each other too often. I was left with joint cus-
tody of our two children and an apartment with a huge (by
Manhattan standards) kitchen that was complete with a
professional cooking range, the latest in refrigeration equipment, and loads of work space. The frustrating problem was
that I didn't know how to cook. I had never planned and put
together an entire dinner, yet I wanted to be able to prepare
meals for the kids and any friends or relatives who might
drop by. I began to stew about this problem until finally a
ten-word target formed in my conscious brain and gave me a
clear-cut direction:

"I want to learn to be an all-around cook."

I began to research the subject by going to bookstores
and checking for basic "neophyte-in-the-kitchen" books. A
spin through *Joy of Cooking* convinced me that I needed to do
more than just *read* recipes, I had to cook them. But I didn't
want to do this as a solo adventure, so next I asked friends
who were good cooks if they could recommend cooking
classes. There were lots of suggestions, ranging from a six-
week Italian cooking course to a twelve-week tour of "Canapé
Preparation." Everything seemed to be overly specialized,
complex graduate courses for the already accomplished
chef. It appeared that there wasn't much need for a cooking class dedicated to the newly divorced, all-thumbs male
who previously had entered the kitchen only to retrieve
beers.

With that realization, I began to generate ideas, and the
key idea happened fast. In a flash it presented itself: I would
start a cooking class right in my own kitchen, and invite any
of my newly divorced male friends who might share this
chef's-hat-and-skillet fantasy. As recycled bachelors, we had
all encountered the phenomenon of the "$200 Saturday-night
date"—the going price in those days for a fancy night out on
the town. Learning to cook at home would be a brilliant alternative to wearing out American Express cards through
heavy usage.

"A great idea," I said smugly to myself. But now I need some way to make it happen." That required a plan, which would of course include persuading someone to teach this course. I needed a roving instructor, an experienced cook who would be willing to travel to my apartment once a week and teach basic cooking to a bunch of oven-dumb bachelors.

The following Saturday night I was out with some friends for dinner—each couple spending the requisite $200—and described the gist of my proposed cooking class.

"I could teach that for you," said Roz, the lively and attractive woman who was on a first date with my friend. Roz explained that she had taken a number of cooking classes but had never taught one. She also had a friend, Laurie, who was an accomplished chef and might like to teach the course with her. The plan took form quickly as Roz, Laurie, and I held a serious planning meeting the following week. Menu planning, individual dishes, foods, supplies, schedules, costs, and the optimum number of students were all discussed for what would be a ten-week "Bachelor Cooking Class." We decided my kitchen could accommodate six students along with the two instructors and an additional person who would continually clean up as we whipped, stirred, and sautéed our way through an evening.

Roz and Laurie would, of course, be paid for their efforts in teaching this ten-week class. Now I had to recruit the five other males who would be willing to pay $300 apiece for this culinary prep school. And that was a job for—you guessed it —*enthusiasm.* I started calling a few friends I thought might potentially be in need of some rudimentary kitchen skills. The conversations that sold my concept went something like this:

■

"Bill, it's going to be great! After this course, you'll be able to cook the *whole* meal while your lady watches TV and smokes cigars."

Bill: "Sign me up."

■

"Alan, we're even going to have one session on preparing an elegant Sunday brunch—including the mandatory Eggs Benedict. You will be a very impressive date."

Alan: "I'm in."

■

"Wayne, the only thing I ever saw you cook was ribs on a barbecue—and even those were burned. This is your chance to become an all-around threat!"

Wayne: "Here's my check."

■

"Dave, drinking will begin at seven P.M. Dinner will be served at eleven P.M. And in between you'll learn to cook. How about it?"

Dave: "I'll be there at seven."

■

"Thayer, imagine telling Ann that you'll prepare the *entire* Thanksgiving dinner next year."

Thayer (the only married candidate): "Ann says to do it."

■

The Monday night cooking class was a huge success with everyone reeling out of my building well after midnight. Tuesday mornings at certain offices around Manhattan may have been bleary events, but in those ten weeks we all learned how to prepare more than fifty different dishes.

New York magazine got wind of this activity and asked to do an article on our weekly food bashes. It appeared as a lively piece entitled "Hey, Good Lookin' . . . What Ya Got Cookin'?" The photo showed our entire group bedecked in aprons, grinning like fools, and posing in front of a table full of delectable Italian masterpieces. The article showed us as graduate cooks, men formerly incompetent around a kitchen who could now actually plan and prepare complete meals. At the course's conclusion, we cleaned our pots, collected our recipes, and journeyed off individually to practice our new-found skills—and to surprise and amaze our legions of doubting friends.

■

I was well equipped to stir up interest in that cooking class. After all, I'd gotten my advanced training in *enthusiasm* a decade earlier. In 1970, I had resigned from the gentlemanly organization that was Young & Rubicam to join a scrappy, medium-sized agency owned by a marketing buzzsaw named Dick Manoff. A health and exercise fanatic, Dick was chock-full of ideas and blessed with a truckload of energy and enthusiasm. There was no question that he *believed* in successful outcomes. If I had a "bachelor's degree" in enthusiasm, Dick had his Ph.D. In great part, I had come to his agency to learn from him.

My job was to run the thirty-person creative department, a gaggle of copywriters, art directors, and television producers. We had a wide range of clients, from Welch's jelly and Bumble Bee tuna to Smith Corona typewriters, National Car Rental and Martell cognac. These clients required a constant diet of new ideas, new campaigns, new thinking. Manoff's input touched everything—the marketing strategies, the research studies, the media plans, the creative concepts, even the production techniques. But his finest hour was always the "new business presentation."

An agency's new business pitch is a frenzied, highly competitive affair. Typically, your shop is fighting for an account with as many as a dozen competitors. All the agencies receive the same briefing from the potential client—and all of them return two or three weeks later to present their ideas and plans. It is, of course, winner-take-all. Even in cases where our agency was the obvious dark horse, Dick Manoff would press on with optimism. His spirit was infectious; our team would pull together and the final presentation usually placed us in the winner's circle or, at the very least, neck and neck with the front runner.

One day, after winning a particularly rough shoot-out, I stuck my head into Dick's corner office and asked, "Do you always believe you're going to succeed?"

It was a question he answered with another question: "Can you possibly imagine beginning a venture by believing you're going to *fail?*"

It may sometimes be easy to develop an original idea. But without enthusiasm, it will be very difficult to make your idea happen. Here is pioneer automaker Walter Chrysler on the subject:

> *The real secret of success is enthusiasm,*
> *Yes, more than enthusiasm,*
> *I would say excitement.*
> *I like to see men get excited.*
> *When they get excited*
> *they make a success of their lives.*
> *You can do anything if you have enthusiasm.*
> *Enthusiasm is the yeast that makes your hope*
> *rise to the stars.*
> *Enthusiasm is the sparkle in your eye,*
> *it is the swing in your gait,*
> *the grip of your hand,*
> *the irresistible surge of your will*
> *and your energy to execute your ideas.*
> *Enthusiasts are fighters.*
> *They have fortitude, they have staying qualities.*
> *Enthusiasm is at the bottom of all progress.*
> *With it there is accomplishment.*
> *Without it there are only alibis.*

If you do not include *enthusiasm* in your arsenal, you are shackling yourself—and handicapping your ideas—dramatically. But don't take my word (or Walter Chrysler's) for that. Ask the next highly successful person you meet what he or she thinks of enthusiasm.

And get ready for a rave review.

Chapter 17

THE WONDERS OF CHUTZPAH

I am a Midwestern WASP. And there is no Midwestern WASP living—including me—who can properly pronounce the word "chutzpah." It is a Yiddish word used to describe people with moxie. With brass. And with a cast-iron ego that allows them to make a spectacle of themselves. P. T. Barnum had chutzpah. Lee Iacocca seems to exhibit the Italian version of chutzpah. And do you remember when Nikita Khrushchev took off his shoe at the United Nations and pounded the table? Russian chutzpah.

Chutzpah is another ingredient that will take you a long way toward making your creative ideas happen. I am not advocating "Crude Chutzpah," the sort exhibited by people who try to get things done by being loud and obnoxious. The reaction is usually extreme: either total surrender or stiffened resistance, neither of which is desirable when you are presenting your ideas. Instead, I would like to sing the praises of "Creative Chutzpah"—the imaginative, daring act that makes people stand back and say, "Wow! How did he pull that off?!"

For many years I've been friendly with a Prince of Chutzpah named Remar Sutton. He's a tall, bald Southerner with an affable disarming charm and an "I'll do anything" approach to getting things done. Remar describes the employment of chutzpah as walking a very fine line. Do it right, and you will be thought of as someone who gets things done with flair and imagination. But slip up just one little bit—and you are a buffoon. Remar has long had one simple objective for his chutzpah: "To become well known as a bright person with courage."

I first met Remar back in 1969 when, at the age of twenty-eight, he joined the New York office of Young & Rubicam. He had wangled a $12,000-a-year job in the traffic department, an administrative "messenger boy" position. Typically, he could expect to be promoted to "assistant account executive" after putting in two long, hard years. All other members of the traffic department were college graduates, many of them with previous experience in the advertising business. Remar fell a little short. He'd dropped out of college before getting a degree—and had absolutely no experience in advertising. In spite of these drawbacks, Remar was determined to shorten his "dues-paying" time dramatically. He said to himself, "I'm in a creative business. How can I demonstrate that I've got what it takes?" How could he prove he had imagination, guts, and the ability to make ideas happen?

During his first week on the job, Remar was assigned to help me with the "Build a park in Harlem" project. I was instantly impressed with his organized approach and brazen ability to pick up the phone and call just about anyone. But Remar kept much of his focus on his own agenda. He'd been at the agency only six weeks when he dreamed up his totally

unprecedented idea: He told me he was going to host a sump-
tuous dinner party and invite every one of the company's top
executives.

Naturally, I said he was crazy. But people had apparently
been telling Remar Sutton that for most of his life; it didn't
stop him for a moment. He charmed a Y&R executive into
donating his home in Connecticut for the evening. He had
formal invitations engraved stating: REMAR SUTTON INVITES
YOU TO AN EVENING OF SOUTHERN DINING. Then he got really
creative. He cajoled a member of the personnel department
into revealing the home addresses of everyone who was a
senior vice president and higher, a list that went up to and
included all members of the board of directors and the agency's chairman. Remar then rented tuxedos for six fellow
members of the traffic department and launched them in
hired limousines on the Saturday a week before the dinner.
Picture this: You're a senior executive of Y&R at home on the
weekend in Greenwich, Connecticut, when a long black
chauffeur-driven limo pulls up your driveway and a tuxedo-
clad messenger steps out bearing an engraved invitation on
a silver tray. He says, "Good afternoon. An invitation from
Remar Sutton," and quietly departs.

Seventy-five invitations were delivered that afternoon.
Most of the recipients must have said, "Who in the world is
Remar Sutton?" And Remar himself began to wonder if he'd
gone too far. His worst fears seemed to be confirmed when,
at 9:05 on Monday morning, the senior vice president respon-
sible for the traffic department appeared at Remar's cubicle
with a fierce scowl. "What the hell are you doing?" he de-
manded. Then he broke into a grin. "But it's a great idea—
and I'll come."

Most of those invited actually attended. Beautiful young
women dressed in Southern-style gowns greeted guests at the
front door with smiles and champagne. The house's furniture
had been removed and low tables with black satin table-
cloths were arranged in various rooms. There were no chairs,
so when senior VPs sat down to dinner, they sat on the floor.
The cuisine was authentically Southern, including bushels of

fresh Savannah crabs flown in that afternoon. The wines were well selected and sublime. The evening went by in an elegant Southern swirl.

Am I making this up? Could this really have happened? After all, Remar Sutton had been working at Y&R about two months. He was a low-paid trainee who hadn't even met most of the people he sent invitations to. And the affair cost $1,200 —10 percent of his annual salary. But I was one of the people who attended that legendary dinner party. And it really did happen.

Remar achieved his objective with amazing speed. The week after the dinner party, the chairman's special assistant came to see him and said, "Anyone who can think up and organize something like that deserves to be in this business." Remar was immediately promoted to account executive (not assistant account executive) and given a $3,000 raise—a spectacular return on his investment of money and chutzpah.

Remar Sutton has long since left Madison Avenue to pursue new—yet always memorable—activities. Today he writes a syndicated column for *The Washington Post*, is a novelist published by the Book-of-the-Month Club, and is a high-profile writer of nonfiction books.

■

The advertising business is a good place to hunt for examples of Creative Chutzpah, the latest example of which may well be a guy named Don Peppers. Don is a hired gun, a man who has moved to three different ad agencies to head up their new business efforts. He's a first-rate marketing thinker who graduated number one in his class at the Air Force Academy. But the thing that earns Don annual compensation rumored to be in excess of $400,000 is his ability to get his foot in the doors of potential clients. Recently, an agency he worked for was in the semifinals for a major retail account, a high-volume "move-'em-out-the-door" consumer electronics chain. When the client cut the list down to six finalists, Don's agency was eliminated. Don called, but the client's decision was firm. The list was closed. Period.

Undeterred, Don learned through an inside source that the company's management group would meet at a hotel in New Jersey the following week to consider presentations from the six finalist agencies. He firmly believed that his agency was more sales-oriented than any of the finalists. So what should he do? It was time for Creative Chutzpah. Of course, this kind of chutzpah must always have a creative purpose. Don started by coming up with his ten-word target: "Prove we'll beat down doors—but do it with grace." Again using his sources, Don found out that the management group meeting in New Jersey had allowed one hour in the middle of the day to have lunch sent in. Hotel food! He could picture the tired cold cuts and damp potato salad. He immediately called the hotel and reserved the meeting room next door to the one that would be used by the management group. Then he began to think about—*pizza!* Who could resist the spicy aroma of hot pizza?

At 11:30 on the appointed day, Don put the rest of his plan into action. Along with his agency's president, he quietly occupied the room they had rented right next to the action. At precisely 12:20, four hot pizzas (two plain, two with everything) were delivered to their room. At 12:30 one of the ad agencies wrapped up its pitch next door and left with their projectors, easels, and presentation boards. Then, as the hotel people started to wheel in little carts of unappetizing food, Don and his president appeared carrying pizza boxes. One of the retail executives sniffed and asked hungrily, "Hey, who ordered the pizza?"

"How do you want it?" Don asked. "Plain or with everything?" A little confused but also hungry, the consumer electronics execs dug in. As they took their first bites, Don introduced the agency president, who told the group they had made a big mistake. "Just give us five minutes while you enjoy the pizza," he said. "After all, we must be pretty good salespeople to have gotten this far." Bowled over and amused by this aggressive approach, the retail executives immediately expanded the finalist list to seven shops. Don's agency was back in the running. Sorry to say, the agency did not ultimately win the account—but at least their agile display of chutzpah got them a chance to be heard.

Creative Chutzpah can give you a memorable advantage. After all, in this competitive world we can all use a way to stand out from the pack. Like the young salesman who, after months of trying, was able to secure a luncheon appointment with the key man at a potentially enormous account. It was a chance to make his career skyrocket—if only our young tiger could suitably impress his important guest. So he went to his boss, a wise old soul, and asked his advice on how to orchestrate a memorable luncheon. And he brought along his pet idea: since the young salesman needed a second car anyway, why not invest in a brand-new Mercedes? Our hero imagined himself showing up in this glistening machine to drive the duly impressed customer to lunch. The sage old sales manager listened, silently recollecting the thousands of sales calls he had made in his career and how very few of those pitches were likely to have been *remembered* by his customers. Then he gave the young man this advice:

"Take the money you would use for that Mercedes and buy a restored 1941 Packard convertible. When you arrive for this appointment, toss your customer the Packard's keys and tell him, 'You drive.' He will never—ever—forget you."

To succeed, Creative Chutzpah must be memorable—a good memory, not a bad one. And to a certain extent, that kind of chutzpah can be learned. But how far can you push yourself to become more memorable? Your stuffy, professional self will, of course, protest mightily. But, in fact, you can probably stretch the "envelope of respectability" a lot further than you might think.

Here's another extreme example to help you keep your

eye on those flamboyant outer fringes. At RJR Nabisco, in the fun-filled days before the Great Takeover of 1988, the company was a loose, profitable place run by a high-profile wizard named Ross Johnson. This controversial executive had a band of top executives he referred to as his "Merry Men." One of them, Peter Rogers, a fast-talking Englishman who fairly crackles with ideas, ran the Nabisco cookie business and was part of the late-night crew that met frequently with Ross Johnson to toss down whiskey and cook up new concepts. After the sudden, traumatic LBO, Rogers opted to take a bundle of cash and retire. But he also wanted to stay in touch with the business, so he continued to attend food industry functions. Often, executives of other companies would ask if he was interested in consulting, and would request a business card. Was Peter Rogers going to use an old RJR card with a new phone number handwritten in? Would he commission a discreet, conservative card proclaiming EXECUTIVE AT LEISURE? Don't be ridiculous. Peter Rogers is a man with English chutzpah!

Herewith (with his permission) is the business card that introduces this iconoclastic food industry executive to his colleagues:

Using Creative Chutzpah to sell your ideas is similar to one of the techniques you used to generate your ideas in the first place: "Go a little bananas." When you start to generate *selling* ideas, begin with the far-out, beyond-the-pale concepts that stretch your imagination. Then, when you pull back to more comfortable concepts, you'll find that, even though reined in, your thoughts and plans will be tinged with chutzpah. So while trying to get your idea out of the oven and onto the table, be enthusiastic, be brave, be inventive, be memorable.

■

Wouldn't it be sad to work somewhere for forty years, retire, and one year later have people asking, "Which one was he?" So muster up your courage and make a little noise. Do something that will stick in people's minds. In short, push yourself to practice chutzpah.

Even if you can't pronounce it.

PART IV

Creativity, Inc. How Business Creates

Chapter 18

THE MILLION-DOLLAR MEETING

The world of business is a place of incessant creative tumult. New problems and new possibilities pop up constantly. There is a continual demand for fresh ideas and innovative approaches. And those who are most skilled at developing ideas—and making them happen—will inevitably rise to the top. Creativity in business is sometimes a Eureka, a breakthrough idea of staggering proportions. But far more often new ideas are modifications, new twists or tweaks that result from a Nibble-Nibble environment. There is a fertile place to nurture this kind of creativity, a meeting that includes a small number of peers who can each bring slightly different experiences to the table. The specific idea will actually be conceived by one mind (*groups* don't think up ideas; they provide grist for an *individual* sitting at the table to think one up). The S.T.R.I.K.E. creative process does work in a group—it is something I like to call "The Million-Dollar Meeting."

The premise of a Million-Dollar Meeting is that even a small idea, if it can save money in the way things are being done presently or can make more money by doing something that isn't being done, will sooner or later return at least one million dollars to the company bottom line. If, for example, someone in a company with fifty salespeople can suggest a way to eliminate some sales forms and simplify all other forms the salespeople fill out, several hours of time might be saved each week. Assume that each hour of a salesperson's time costs the company $100 and that two hours a week can be saved by this one move. That's $200 a week multiplied by fifty-two weeks times the company's fifty salespeople. That works out to $520,000 in one year and more than a million dollars in two years. Of course, this tactic could have a far greater impact on profits since it would allow each salesperson to *sell* for an extra two hours every week.

Here's an example of creative group thinking. In 1989, I was in a meeting with Jet Aviation, the world's largest company chartering business jets—they are the "Hertz" of jet rental. We were trying to think up ideas to increase the volume of calls for charter service and were pinning concepts up on the wall. Our advertising campaign included newspaper ads, ads in aviation trade magazines, and Yellow Pages ads, all of which carried a toll-free "800" number to be dialed when a customer needed a jet and crew. But the number they had was a jumble of digits that no one, not even the company's own president could remember. Someone suggested we simplify the telephone number by finding an acronym. However, in any marketing category, most of the obvious numbers are gone—having been taken years back by the "800" number pioneers. If you sell beer wholesale, you will probably find that 1-800 BUY BEER is no longer available. A used car lot that wants 1-800 USED CAR is almost certainly out of luck. The result of this scarcity has forced many marketers to concoct those weird, unmemorable acronyms like 1-800-54BEER9.

"Why don't we try to get 1-800 RENT JET?" I said jokingly. "Unless it was taken by the Wright Brothers." But then someone called to make sure it was out of reach. Incredibly, the number was available—and we immediately reserved it. Today, any secretary who wants to rent a jet for the boss need only remember 1-800 RENT JET and start dialing. In time— even though it may take years—that one simple concept will have returned one million dollars in revenue. That's what a Million-Dollar Meeting is all about: Think of a simple idea, put it into action, and give it time.

My advertising agency serves two large clients in the magazine business, *Newsweek* and *Reader's Digest*, each of which has an advertising sales department that is a marketing juggernaut; well over a hundred sales and marketing support people all dedicated to selling ad pages. I have used the principles of S.T.R.I.K.E. at meetings with both *Newsweek* and *Reader's Digest*. Here's an example of how it works. Late in 1990, a small group of *Newsweek* executives decided to meet to discuss ideas for promoting the magazine's "ahead of the curve" editorial coverage to the advertising community. It was the first time we would try this kind of idea-generation session, and we had decided upon a specific ten-word target to explore:

"Make Newsweek more visible to ad agency and advertiser executives."

We limited this 8 A.M. breakfast meeting to five people: Rick Smith, the magazine's editor in chief; Peter Eldredge, the U.S. publisher; two senior marketing executives; and myself as the designated "idea scribe." We met in a small conference room and I had brought along a big pad of paper and a roll of masking tape (Rick Smith arrived a few minutes late, having been delayed by traffic). We began by writing out and posting the ten-word target. As ideas began to flow, I quickly sketched the essence of each idea, added the identifying words, and posted it on the wall. The magic began to happen, and the wall was soon covered with ideas. In less than an hour we generated ideas ranging from unique mailing pieces promoting the special perspective of the editors on world events and videos based on special issues of the magazine to in-depth breakfast briefings for key customers on the Gulf crisis (which dominated most cover stories during the fourth quarter of 1990). Eighteen specific ideas were conceived and

Idea sketches can be crudely done and need only a minimum of descriptive words.

sketched in less than sixty minutes, and they were all up there in plain sight for everyone to see, respond to, and be stimulated by. As we wrapped up the session, editor Rick Smith said, "This was fun. I'll be on time for the next one of these."

With S.T.R.I.K.E. as a reminder of all the bases you have to touch, you can turn any creative confab into a Million-Dollar Meeting ("MDM" for short). Here's how you can set up an MDM. First of all, you should alert the key people concerned that you want to address a particular problem. State that problem in the form of a ten-word target and circulate it among the group along with the time and place of the meeting. Give everybody time to stew a bit about the problem and do their homework—research—before the meeting. Next, choose a meeting room where dozens of ideas can be pinned up on the wall, and make sure it is well stocked with pads of paper and felt-tip markers. When the group gathers at the appointed time—and it's best if you keep idea-generation groups to less than a dozen people—restate the problem clearly. Take a big sheet of paper, boldly letter your ten-word target on it, and pin it to the wall. Before you begin, you might want to ask each person to write the words "I WON'T BE NEGATIVE" on a scrap of paper—and then sit on it. Then, if someone starts to suggest that an idea won't work or that it's been tried before, or complains that it is just plain dumb, ask the wet blanket to stand and read the piece of paper on his or her chair. It usually requires only one public recitation to keep a group on track.

To run a successful "MDM," you should pay particular attention to *The Four Gives:*

> **(1)** Give the target.
> **(2)** Give permission to play.
> **(3)** Give praise.
> **(4)** Give credit.

As the group leader, you start off by (1) giving the target —and posting it in clear sight. You continue by eliminating the negative and (2) giving everyone permission to play, the license to say whatever comes to mind. It's great fun to be encouraged to be playful with business problems, and as the session gets under way, you should start (3) giving praise. Everybody loves public praise, so try to find something encouraging to say about every single contribution. Load it on. After all, nothing pleases the human animal more than being complimented on original thinking. A genuinely felt "Good idea, Bill" far surpasses the parking-lot comment "Great-looking car, Bill" or even a shouted "Terrific shot, Bill!" at the company golf match. Once an idea has been offered, visualize it in words and pictures on a piece of paper, pin it on the wall, and keep going. Your praise will keep the idea wheels greased and a dozen egos keenly involved.

Finally—and this usually takes place after the meeting—you (4) give credit. Always give generous credit to the person who actually thought up an original idea, and also to anyone who may have "tweaked" an idea to make it better. In some future meeting with *your* bosses, if you can honestly say, "Here's a super idea that Lois thought of . . ." you will have permanently endeared yourself to your creative team. But just once steal credit for yourself, and you can forget about any more exciting idea-generation sessions—not only that, you will surely have to worry about Lois giving her next idea to a new organization. If we added three more "Gives" to the list shown above, they would read: (5) GIVE CREDIT, (6) GIVE CREDIT, and (7) GIVE CREDIT.

During the meeting, as the ideas begin to flow, one person (the best scribbler in the pack) should act as the meeting's "cartoonist," quickly sketching, labeling, and pinning the ideas to the wall. This is critical to the process. If, instead, a scribe simply *writes down* each idea on a pad of yellow paper, you will witness the instantaneous birth and death of tiny idea fragments. Once the next idea is mentioned, the previous idea has lost its moment on the stage. It's gone! The idea disappears into the mist—and its ability to serve as inspiration for ideas to follow has been dramatically handicapped. But when ideas are represented on the wall, they remain pactive contributors to the meeting. There is a creative ex-

citement that builds as more and more idea sketches adorn
the wall. A subtle competition even begins to emerge ("Gee,
Lois has three ideas up there and I haven't come up with
even one yet . . ."). With lots of "attaboys" and "attagirls,"
you can push the group to "Mix, Match, and Plus" the ideas
on the wall. Idea Democracy is declared with all participants
encouraged to hitchhike on any idea that anyone else has
proposed.

In a creative meeting I usually declare a break after about
an hour. Everyone leaves and a time is scheduled to recon-
vene, perhaps the next day. This pause allows the participants to do some more stewing and more research, and give
more thought to their ideas. It also allows "Look/Don't Look/
Look" insights to happen when the group returns to the room
and looks at the previous day's sketches still posted on the
wall. Almost immediately new hunches will blossom into a
new batch of concepts. Keep going until the walls are over-
flowing with ideas. Be a cheerleader for quantity; the more
ideas, the merrier the meeting. It may take two sessions—or
three—but eventually you must begin to sort through all the
possibilities and, with the group's help, pick the key idea, the
one that will hit your target squarely. Keep the runners-up
to stimulate ideas for next month's meeting. Then appoint
someone as godfather or godmother to the anointed idea, the
person best able to make it happen. Give that person a clear
assignment to put that idea into motion. Give that person
all the resources he or she needs. And give that person a *due
date.*

■

I have been successfully using these techniques in creative
meetings for over twenty years. Do they work? Yes. Will your
group generate ideas that you can put into action? Yes. Will
any of them be "million-dollar ideas"? Sooner or later, yes.
If you regularly convene a "Million-Dollar Meeting," you will
unleash a creative power in your organization that may
amaze you. Your people will see their own creativity take
physical form—the paper on the wall. They will feel the con-

tributions they are making to the company, and they will know that they count. Even if a particular idea didn't get selected this month, each person knows there's another meeting coming up next month. Most of all, your people will be *turned on* to the idea of generating ideas and making them happen.

Chapter 19

CREATIVITY
AND CLAIRVOYANCE

Possibly the most spectacular examples of creativity in business spring from what I call "business clairvoyance," the ability to see something no one else seems to see. Sometimes an idea doesn't even need to be invented; it just needs to be recognized and *utilized*. For example, Sir William Stephenson, the British spy who was the hero of the best-seller *A Man Called Intrepid*, had outstanding business clairvoyance. During World War I (in his pre-spy days), he was a pilot for the RAF and shot down twenty-six enemy planes—until one of them got him. Captured when his plane crashed, he was locked up in a German prisoner-of-war camp. There he noticed an ingenious can opener that the guards were using.

None of the other prisoners thought it was anything special, but Stephenson was fascinated by the device. He managed to escape from the camp and take one of the can openers with him. Back in England he did some research and discovered that the can opener had been patented only in Germany. After the war he adapted the can opener's design, obtained worldwide patents, and built a fortune on it. He also invented many things from scratch, including the first device for sending photographs by radio, and—in his spare time—won the European lightweight boxing championship.

Business clairvoyance is rarely that simple. Usually the "can opener" isn't just handed to you. More often the elements of an idea are just sitting around, but everyone else overlooks them. The business clairvoyant has learned to recognize two or more disparate pieces of information, then put them together for the first time.

■

Al Ueltschi is an American swashbuckler. In the 1930s he learned to fly and became one of those steely-eyed pilots who eked out a living barnstorming. He flew his beat-up open-cockpit biplane from county fair to county fair, giving two-dollar rides and performing thrilling aerobatic displays. One day it became particularly thrilling. Al's plane was upside down in a maneuver called the half snap roll. Suddenly his seat broke loose from the airplane's flimsy floorboard and he and the seat fell out at 3,000 feet above ground. Before pulling the ripcord on his parachute, he had to unbelt himself from the seat and push it away. That took a few seconds; he was down to 1,500 feet and falling fast. He then grasped for his chute, which finally billowed open at about 200 feet up (from there you can almost count the blades of grass) to barely cushion the impact. That incident must have cleared his head permanently for the business clairvoyance he would soon demonstrate.

By the late 1940s, Ueltschi had spent a few years as a pilot for Pan American and had learned—as do all airline pilots—that you do not get enough training by flying routine missions every day. Also known to government officials, this realization led to the establishment of special refresher training courses emphasizing emergency situations. In its new watchdog role, the Department of Commerce passed a ruling requiring that commercial airline pilots undergo such training twice a year. Meanwhile, something else was happening in aviation: America's fast-growing corporations were discovering the convenience of corporate airplanes. Amalgamated Flower Baskets Inc., for example, would buy a war surplus C-47 transport plane and hire two pilots to fly it. Typically, both of these flyboys would have flown over fifty missions during the war. Wearing nifty leather jackets, they knew *everything* about flying that C-47. But there was no government agency that required these "business pilots" to take refresher training. Surely, thousands of people in aviation saw what was happening. Except they *didn't* see what was happening:

(1) Commercial airline pilots were required to take regular refresher training to stay sharp on their emergency procedures.

(2) Business pilots were *not* required to take it.

"This is odd," thought Al Ueltschi. "There's an idea for a business here." He became obsessed with his concept for a company offering refresher training to the growing cadre of business pilots. But he didn't have the money he needed to start this company. Or did he? Al put together a written proposal and went to call on the recently formed flight departments of Eastman Kodak and National Distillers. He talked about the safety of executive passengers, and about the need to practice certain very dangerous emergency situations in a flight simulator—not aloft in the airplane. "How can you 'practice' an engine fire when you're up flying in the C-47?" he asked. The executives were impressed.

Then Ueltschi did something very creative. He asked the companies to *advance* him the first six months' fee for training their pilots. Guess what? They were so impressed with Ueltschi's idea—and energy—they wrote the checks. He then mortgaged his house to get some additional funds and bought his first crude flight simulator. He hired a couple of part-time instructors, rented some space at La Guardia Airport, and in 1951 a company called FlightSafety International was born. Al kept the pressure on. He pushed, prodded, yelled profanities at, and even cajoled (not in his nature) his gradually expanding staff. Late every night he would sit down at an old typewriter and crank out a dozen letters to corporate airplane owners. And little by little, simulator by simulator, the company grew.

If you had invested $10,000 in FlightSafety stock in 1968 you would be a happier person today; your holdings would be worth in the neighborhood of $1 million. FlightSafety is now the world's largest training company. It offers high-technology simulator training for business pilots, military pilots, and a growing number of commercial pilots. Even pilots who fly the president of the United States now take some of their refresher training at FlightSafety. Spinoff ventures include simulators for nuclear power plant operators and the crews of marine supertankers. At the age of 73, Al is still on the job every day—still yelling colorful profanities—and is rapidly becoming America's newest billionaire. Al Ueltschi, who recognized a need and filled it, is a very creative man.

■

If clairvoyance is the ability to see something others cannot see, then John Evans is a clairvoyant. An Englishman in his early fifties who always seems to be moving at 110 miles an hour, John has a passion for fast cars (was a Formula II race car driver in his younger years) and fast talk. His eyes glint with humor as he shoots out rapid-fire comments, questions, and ideas. He has little patience for clichés or mundane thinking.

John has earned his way into media mogul Rupert Murdoch's inner circle of top managers. Murdoch's company, News America Publishing Inc., has proven to be a very creative place. Memos and meetings are minimized. Decisions are often made when two people pass each other in the hall. And ten-million-dollar proposals can actually be approved with a sixty-second phone call to Rupert Murdoch. In 1985, John Evans was president of Murdoch Magazines, running the division that included three well-established publications, *New York* magazine, *The Village Voice,* and the weekly tabloid *The Star.* The group had also recently completed successful launches of the movie magazine *Premiere,* a car buff publication named *Automobile,* and a new entry into the highly competitive area of women's magazines, *New Woman.* Evans probably had enough on his plate to keep the average company president working a sixty-hour week. But that year Rupert Murdoch decided to invest $350 million to acquire from Ziff-Davis a group of travel industry publications and directories, along with some aviation trade magazines. They all got dumped into John Evans's group.

Evans wanted to focus on the travel category and immediately got Murdoch's approval to sell off the aviation publications for what was rumored to be about $65 million. Then he took a look at what remained. The centerpiece of the travel publications was the travel industry's "bible," a telephone-book-sized directory called the *Hotel & Travel Index.* Invaluable to a travel agent, it lists pertinent information on most of the world's hotels, motels, and resorts. Going to Cairo? This directory describes the places to stay, phone and fax numbers, price and type of rooms, alternative meal plans, and what credit cards they take.

Evans began to think about the travel business and how it had changed. During the forties and fifties, it was a business where travel agents *sold* their clients by suggesting trips they might take. There weren't that many places to go. Destinations were restricted by the practical limitations of piston-powered commercial airliners. It took almost five hours of flying just to get from New York to Miami. As a result, the knowledgeable travel agent could, after a few years in the business, have personally visited most of the popular destinations. He could sell a client on the virtues of Puerto Rico or Paris because he'd been there.

Then, in the late fifties, everything changed. The Boeing 707 arrived. Suddenly high-speed jet travel opened up thousands of new destinations to the family with a few bucks to spend and a one-week vacation to enjoy. At the same time the travel industry expanded and young people flocked to become travel agents. But these inexperienced kids hadn't personally seen most of the world's pleasure spots—and now, there were so many more places you could get to. For example, in 1960, Cancún, Mexico, was nothing but a sand spit; today it hosts millions of tourists annually. In 1970, Orlando's Walt Disney World was a swamp. Jet planes made it—and hundreds of other new tourist meccas—accessible. The kids in the travel business were overwhelmed; they were reluctant to "sell" a client on a trip they hadn't experienced themselves. As a result, they became a legion of order takers.

"How can we get travel agents to sell again?" Evans wondered. In the deep recesses of his brain, business clairvoyance began to bubble. He owned the industry's most valued reference book. Weighing fourteen pounds a copy, *Hotel & Travel Index* is a gigantic data base. It contains thousands of large, gray, type-filled pages. What if he could bring this information to life? Could the index be married to some new technology? Were the elements of an idea lying here just waiting to be recognized?

Evans had a vision—of vision. He would develop a visual data base and put it on a computer monitor placed on every travel agent's desk. "You're interested in Morocco?" an agent could ask a client, then turn to the computer keyboard. "Here's the Hotel El Grandioso [a photo comes up on the monitor] and this is what a master suite looks like." If the client plays tennis, the agent can show a picture of the tennis court. Is the El Grandioso too expensive? The computer monitor can display other hotels in Morocco that offer tennis. "And while we're at it, let's just pull up a city map and take a look at weather patterns this time of year." And if the client wants the pictures, maps, and rainfall chart to take home, hard copies can be printed out on a laser-printer.

All customer data would also be contained in the com-

puter. Evans went on to imagine a time in the future when the computer would tell the agent in January that "The Smith family took a one-week vacation to Florida last April and spent $1,800 for airfare and lodging." Based on its programmed-in knowledge of the Smith family's past travel preferences, the computer would then go on to make some educated guesses about where they might like to go this year. It would come up with three separate suggestions; Plans A and B would cost about the same as last year's trip, Plan C might be somewhat more luxurious. Since the computer would know the present ages of the children, it could figure out the right combination of rooms and suggest places with activities they might enjoy. Finally, it could print out pictures of the hotels, room views, and sports facilities, as well as local maps, for each of the three plans. And guess what America's travel agents could do with these personalized, customized brochures? They could actually make a *sales call.*

That was the concept: pictures that sell, a grand idea that occurred to John Evans when his brain melded a decades-old printed directory and the new graphic, digital power of the computer. But, of course, the story had just begun. Clairvoyance had done its thing. John had gone through S.T.R.I.K. and had the key idea. But the "E," the Execution, of this ambitious brainstorm, remained to be accomplished.

Fortunately, John has a lot of enthusiasm, even chutzpah. He *made his idea happen.* He began by calling in fifteen travel agents from around the country. He swore them to secrecy, put a copy of the *Hotel & Travel Index* on the table, then asked, "If I were to turn this book into an electronic machine, what would it look like? What would it do?" It was a question he would continue to ask for the next four years. Simultaneously, he began to build his visual data base with a massive mailing to hotels and lodging places worldwide. The response that came from 45,000 hotels included 140,000 images and at least ninety pieces of information on each hotel. Then John persuaded Rupert Murdoch to invest an additional $45 million to buy two companies to set up the program and input his mountain of graphic data. He personally negotiated with the seventeen largest national hotel chains to get them on line with his new system, now named JAGUAR. Next he tackled a highly resistant airline industry, which wanted to handle hotel reservations on its own sophisticated computer reservations systems in order to keep the sales commissions the activity generated. Ultimately the airlines capitulated; they couldn't compete with the massive, growing data base of graphic information Evans's exotic machine contained. The airlines grimaced, then signed on with JAGUAR. A new giant had suddenly loomed up in the travel business.

Rupert Murdoch is a businessman. On July 1, 1989, he sold JAGUAR and the travel publications. Why? Here's the math. Murdoch originally invested $350 million but sold off his aviation publications for something like $65 million. He then spent another $45 million. That's a total of $330 million invested. JAGUAR was sold to Reed International for $860 million. In just four years, John Evans had created and executed an idea worth over half a billion dollars in profit.

Today, John continues to think broadly—and profitably—

for the Murdoch organization. It's not bad duty for a "business clairvoyant."

■

Can you put clairvoyance to work on the job? Think about where your company is going. Then think broadly about the various obvious—and the not-so-obvious—technologies that could help it get there. With some creative stewing and some diligent research, you just might come up with a key idea and make it happen. You don't need a crystal ball to become a clairvoyant. All you need is S.T.R.I.K.E.

Chapter 20

RISKS AND REWARDS

Creative people are risk takers. And exercising creativity within the world of business always brings with it some degree of risk. Often the risk is quite small, the corporate equivalent of the raised eyebrow ("That newfangled delivery schedule Perkins concocted is giving the drivers some headaches . . ."). But why should the corporate newcomer, whose innovative acts tend to be the Nibble-Nibble sort of creativity, worry? After all, the costs of an incremental improvement are normally not staggering. A failure will not threaten the balance sheet, nor will it even show up as a footnote on the monthly P&L statement. What's the risk?

The problem can be that in many corporations a miscued

nibble will slow down a young executive's advancement ("Perkins isn't getting it. Can't seem to go along with how we do things here."), or it can even nudge the boss into suggesting some résumé typing ("Perkins, perhaps you might find some other employer more open to your suggestions . . ."). Since America's big corporations have tended to be rule-heavy, by-the-book operations, you *could* opt to play it safe, do as you're told, and get promoted to your boss's job when he or she—by playing it safe—is promoted to his or her boss's job. So why not just stifle the wacko ideas and make a safe, dull march up the organization chart?

Why not? Because that is yesterday's scenario. In the calm old days, the wishy-washy would rise to middle management, get stuck there, and wait peacefully for retirement. Those days are over. The 1980s put the fear of LBO into managerial hearts and—with or without an actual takeover on the horizon—companies began to pare down the executive ranks. In this new reality, the first to go are the "yes-men" and "yes-women," the stolid ranks of this-is-the-way-it's-done-here corporate plodders. The 1990s are demanding new thinking, new ideas. International competition surrounds us, and anybody, anywhere might just knock off your product, possibly making it better and cheaper. It's going to be a tough job just to keep up with Japan and the newly blossoming creativity of countries like Korea, Taiwan, and the reunited Germany. Americans can no longer sit smugly back, content in the belief that, after all, we are the world's best innovators.

■

In an interview with IBM chief John Akers, I brought up the issue of worldwide creative competition. Although he felt that Americans were skilled at Eureka creativity, Akers unequivocally identified the Japanese as "the world champions at Nibble-Nibble." The message is clear: The United States needs more creative people—which means it needs more risk takers.

Do you want to get ahead? Take risks: little risks at first, bigger risks when you begin to move up. As you are promoted, there will be fewer layers of people above you to water down—or divert—your ideas. As a natural evolution your own creative power will mushroom. You will have more ideas, more confidence, and fewer nay-sayers to brush aside. If you eventually become a world-class creative CEO, you will be a tiger on the subject of ideas. You will set up your organization to foster creativity, search your organization for the best ideas, the best people. You will glorify those ideas and generously reward the people who thought them up. You will quickly forgive the idea-maker who flops ("Nice try, Perkins. Give it another shot!"). Your company will become well known as an extraordinarily creative place. And the most creative people will flock to work there.

An interesting phenomenon inevitably occurs when a risk taker rises in a corporation. As your creative power increases, the risk escalates exponentially. Early in a corporate career, the idea-maker's risk is usually limited to playing "You Bet Your Job." However, at the pinnacle of corporate success, you may be invited to step up to the high-stakes table. You may be challenged to play for the ultimate bundle: *Betting the company.*

Industries change. Companies change. Products change. And once every decade or so, members of a company's top management may have their backs against the wall and be forced to play for the very highest stakes. They ask, "Will this company continue to exist?" and then hand you the dice. It will take great courage to play that game—and supreme confidence. But does it all depend on luck? Nonsense! A creative executive would never, ever leave everything in the fickle hands of Lady Luck. He is willing to take the ultimate risk, but not a stupid ultimate risk. With the power of S.T.R.I.K.E., the odds are weighted in your favor. You're playing with a pair of loaded dice.

■

The Gillette Company operates with a long-established target: *"Make the best wet-shaving razor in the world."* By the late 1980s, that objective had led the company from the early double-edged razor blades to the first twin-blade Trac II system, and on to the improved Atra and Atra Plus twin-blade systems. But something was happening in the wet-shaving business that was depressing profits: the huge growth of low-margin plastic disposable razors. Once used by only a small number of men, the trend to these flimsy throwaways was becoming a stampede. Why? Research showed that women worried about cutting themselves when changing blades in their razors; they far preferred the disposables they could toss away when dull. And when the wife brought a package of disposables home, her husband would grab one or two for himself rather than shop for new replacement blades.

This trend had allowed disposables to capture over 50 percent of the market and, as market leader, Gillette was selling millions of them every day.

But everyone was selling disposables; they had become almost a commodity product and were not very profitable, which tended to depress Gillette's earnings and stock price. That, in turn, attracted the interest of corporate raiders like Revlon owner Ronald O. Perelman. In 1987 he had aggressively offered $4.1 billion for the company but was fended off by Gillette management. In 1988 another raider tried to gain control of the company. This time management promised stockholders that a secret new technology would create more value in the long run than the immediate sale of the company to an outsider.

A secret new technology? Gillette scientists had discovered how to make blades far narrower than ever before. They wanted these flexible new blades to "float" across the face, each blade mounted on its own independent spring. But how could these narrow little blades be attached to springs? Glue didn't work. Other methods proved fruitless. Finally, after a massive creative effort, the Gillette team invented a way for lasers to make the thirteen tiny spot welds needed in each little twin blade cartridge. It was breakthrough technology; each blade was now attached to its own cushioning spring. The result was a noticeably superior shave. With the technology under control, wise heads now turned to marketing.

Since disposables were such an important part of the market, management was recommending that the company follow conventional wisdom. This new razor—dubbed Sensor— should be introduced in both disposable and permanent steel-handle versions.

Enter the voice of dissent. John Symons had been heading up Gillette's European operations and had long held the opinion that disposables were not good for the company's health. One day he walked into a meeting with Gillette's chairman, Coleman Mockler, Jr., and tossed a plastic disposable onto the conference table. As it landed with a flimsy, plinking sound, he asked, "Is *that* what the Gillette Company is going to become?" Symons was already famous within the company for standing up at sales meetings and demanding to know of the assembled, "Are you a plastic man? Or a *steel* man?" Putting his money where his mouth was, Symons had deemphasized disposables in the European markets he managed and had seen profits improve as a result.

Here was top management's dilemma. The company had just elbowed out Perelman and another raider, and some stockholders were grumbling about the money they could have made from a sale. The company was investing more than $200 million in Sensor. Surely the safer course would be to opt for lower profit margins and introduce Sensor— Gillette's first new blade in thirteen years—in both the steel-handle form and the disposable form that almost half of American men were now using.

Was it time to take a risk? To bet the company? An unsuccessful Sensor launch would undoubtedly have caused great discontent among the stockholders and spurred the return of black-hat raiders. In spite of these risks, Gillette's chairman decided they were steel men. Symons was brought in from Europe to launch Sensor and—amid gasps from meeker souls—he immediately killed development of the disposable Sensor. Introduced to American shavers in January 1990, the Sensor is available *only* in the hefty, steel-handle model.

John Symons took a big risk. And it looks as if he rolled a

winning seven. So far, Sensor is a runaway success. For the first few months, drugstores continually ran out of the replacement Sensor blades, a sure sign that users were coming back for more. In its first eight months, Sensor sold the entire year's planned production—and captured a 9 percent share of the market.

■

Allen Paulson is a risk taker. This former aircraft mechanic–turned–entrepreneur is the driving force (and a major owner) of Gulfstream Aerospace, the company that turns out the sleek Gulfstream IV corporate jet. At the age of sixty-eight, Paulson is still energetically—and creatively—running his company. With offices located at the Savannah airport, Paulson has his own helicopter pad out front and early each morning touches down in the jet-powered chopper he flies himself. He also flies his company's Gulfstream jets, accumulating hundreds of hours of flying time each year. This involvement with his airplanes leads to constant improvements; Paulson frequently opens his eyes at 4 A.M. to jot down some new "tweak" that will make things work better.

Long before Paulson was involved, the Grumman Corporation designed and built the original Gulfstream aircraft as a twin-engine turbo prop. It followed this propellor model with a jet version, designated the Gulfstream II. However, Grumman balked at the expense—and risks—inherent in building an improved Gulfstream III. Was the market ready for such an expensive jet? Grumman didn't think so. So in 1978, Paulson stepped in and offered to buy its executive jet division. Grumman breathed a sigh of relief and accepted the offer. Paulson immediately began working on, and improving (Nibble-Nibble), the designs that ultimately led to the bigger, faster Gulfstream III model. The plane was an immediate hit, producing substantial profits for Paulson's new venture.

But things move quickly in the airplane business. As the 1980s began, there was need for a radical change in the engines; airport environmental regulations tightened and became increasingly tough on noise. In order to operate into the country's major airports, the next Gulfstream jet would have to be quieter to satisfy local regulations, and also more efficient to add the almost-5,000-mile range that Paulson envisioned for his next generation of aircraft. This would be a neat trick, since when you muffle an engine, you tend to make it *less* efficient.

Paulson got in touch with the head of Rolls-Royce, the company that was building his engines, and arranged a "Christmas lunch" in December 1982. He sat down with Ralph Robins, who today is the chairman of Rolls-Royce, and outlined his dreams for the Gulfstream IV. It would be the most powerful and luxurious Gulfstream yet—and also the quietest. About the time coffee was served, Paulson asked for a commitment from Rolls-Royce to develop and produce this new engine in time to meet the aircraft delivery dates he had in mind. Robins hesitated, then said no. The enormous research and development costs involved in building this new superengine were simply too daunting. Rolls-Royce would take a pass.

Paulson needed those engines. Without them his company would lose the reputation for leadership and prestige that had been carefully built for years. But when it came to developing an all-new engine, Ralph Robins was not willing to take the financial risk. Fortunately, Allen Paulson was.

"How about if I relieve you on that risk?" he asked of his guest.

"What do you mean?" Robins replied.

Paulson took out a 3 x 5 card and wrote a contract on it. He would commit to buy 400 engines from Rolls-Royce at $1,250,000 per engine—a total commitment of half a billion dollars. Paulson signed the card and passed it to Robins. Most half-billion-dollar contracts weigh several pounds, number hundreds of pages, and have been reviewed by a battalion of lawyers before either side is allowed to sign. Knowing this, Robins paused. He stared at the little 3 x 5 card—a very *powerful* 3 x 5 card. And then he signed it.

A Powerful 3 x 5 Card

Later, when Paulson was asked why the percentages on
the contract added up to 102 percent, he responded, "That's
what happens when you have a two-martini lunch." But even
if slightly miscalculated, that half-billion-dollar card set an
enormous corporate effort into motion. A state-of-the-art
power plant, the Rolls-Royce Tay engine, was successfully
developed and produced, allowing Paulson to build his new
Gulfstream IV and maintain his airplane's top-of-the-hill
image in boardrooms, annual meeting rooms, and country
club locker rooms. There are new challenges looming on the

horizon for Paulson, as he is now planning a joint venture with the Russians to build the first corporate SST (Tokyo to San Francisco in four hours). This skyrocket will cost over $50 million per airplane. And it will be the first American plane built with *Russian supersonic technology*. Sound pretty risky?

It's just everyday stuff for a world-class risk taker.

Chapter 21

BILLIONAIRES

According to *Forbes* maga-zine, in 1990 the United States continued to hold the world lead in the billionaire head count. The United States had 62 billionaires, followed by Japan with 40 billionaires and West Germany with 38. It's hard to imagine a billion dollars. So here's a simple visual exercise: close your eyes and imagine a single bill in the denomination of $1,000,000. Now imagine *one thousand* of these million-dollar bills divided up into three little stacks. Put a rubber band around each stack and reach for an empty cigar box. The three stacks of bills will fit snugly into it.

That's what a billionaire has: one cigar box.

Forbes lists only 13 billionaires who got most of their wealth from inheritance. The other 49 made it themselves. The question is: *How?*

In the process of researching creativity, I met with and interviewed two self-made billionaires, corporate raider Harold Simmons and the young founder of Microsoft, Bill Gates. Each man is incredibly focused. Each has confidence, courage, and energy. And each is able to examine the conventional ways things get done, then break rules, innovate, and —with a lot of coaxing, pushing, and shoving—make something new happen.

Harold Simmons has a simple ten-word target: *"Before I die I expect to be worth ten billion."* Born in Texas, he grew up during the thirties and forties living in a small house outside Dallas that had no running water or toilets. He worked his way through the University of Texas at Austin and graduated with a Phi Beta Kappa key. He tried banking for a while but soon discovered he didn't much like working for other people. So in 1961, Simmons bought a single drugstore with a cash down payment of $5,000. It wasn't all his money; he borrowed some of it. He ran that drugstore profitably, flipping hamburgers and pouring Cokes at the lunch counter, and began to dream of building a chain of drugstores. By leveraging his minuscule capital, he was able to buy even more drugstores. He ran those profitably and leveraged again to buy even more drugstores. After twelve years he owned a hundred drugstores and, in 1973, sold them to Jack Eckerd Corporation for $50 million worth of Eckerd stock.

During the next two years, his stock plummeted in value to $12 million. But strong-willed billionaires-to-be don't let financial body blows slow them down. Simmons began his career-long hunt for companies that are undervalued, doing his research by reading the same business magazines and newspapers you and I can pick up at any newsstand. By studying these conventional sources, he has consistently been able to sleuth out companies that have valuable assets hidden away on their balance sheets, assets the stock market is overlooking. When he finds a gem, he begins to buy the undervalued stock, trying for a majority of the voting shares. Upon achieving control, Simmons typically retains the existing managers, sells any unnecessary assets to help fund the investment he has just made, and works with management to point the company down a new, more profitable path. That done, he picks up *Fortune*, *Forbes*, or *Business Week* to hunt for his next quarry.

Harold Simmons does not allow himself a common conceit, the belief that he is a "Renaissance man" able to generate effective ideas across the broad range of human experience. He restricts his creativity to the thing he knows best—takeover financing. It's a world-class minefield where every potential attack can involve a dizzying combination of conventional financial instruments, freshly invented financial instruments, a few financial feints and ploys, and some hardball corporate psychology. Simmons keeps his creative energy totally focused on new ways to improve his hand. If it's not financial in nature, he'll take a pass. I asked him if, when sitting down with a newly acquired company's managers, he might offer an opinion on their new product ideas. "I pay little attention to product," he replied.

Simmons is also a creative loner. While he has a small staff—and relies on them to help *evaluate* his ideas—he goes it alone when gathering his information, sifting through it, then generating his ideas out driving and singing on the Dallas freeways. You don't get the feeling that Simmons has ever asked for much help in the creative area. He's very happy being a one-man show.

■

Unlike Simmons, William Gates III tries hard *not* to be a one-man show. At Microsoft, the Seattle-based computer software giant Gates founded in 1974, creativity is more like a three-ring circus. Fresh ideas pop out of every office in the place. And in the middle of the action is Bill Gates, the math-genius ringmaster, prodding his people along with a childlike gee-whiz manner that can snap-roll into adultlike cranky criticism if he doesn't like the ideas he sees parading into his center ring.

Gates is a tall, gangly thirty-five-year-old *The Wall Street Journal* has described as "the single most influential figure in the computer industry." In the seventies, he was just another kid getting an allowance and studying at Harvard; by 1991, his stock holdings in Microsoft gave him a net worth of over $4 billion (in other words, he's working on his fifth cigar box). That wealth was built by starting a company that reflects a unique partnership of marketing and product creativity. Having studied how other corporations worked (or didn't work), Gates set up Microsoft with three goals in mind:

(1) As CEO, he would clearly communicate what the company was trying to do.
(2) He would hire great people.
(3) He would allow them to shine—individually.

While abiding with the general principles of a ten-word target, Gates was able to distill the company's mission statement down to a mere eight words: *"Put a world of information at everyone's fingertips."* As it turned out, this target would apply no matter whether the software developer was working on a basic spreadsheet program, a complex scheduling program, or even a sophisticated new graphic information program like Windows 3.0. When it comes to creativity, Gates understands that creative people like to work with other creative people. As a result, Microsoft is an organization that positively glorifies the creative process, and the industry's best software developers have flocked to join the company's swelling ranks.

What's it like to work at Microsoft? Let's invent a twenty-eight-year-old hotshot named Lulu LaRue. Lulu has been working at another software company and has earned the reputation as a terrific "code jockey," which means she's pretty swift when it comes to thinking up and writing the complicated software codes that tell the computer what to do. Microsoft has lured Lulu to the Seattle area with a salary of $45,000 plus stock options—and the opportunity to work on some leading-edge software development. She has rented a small, attractive apartment close to Microsoft's suburban Seattle "campus" and commutes to work on her mountain bike.

In one of the sleek, two-story campus buildings, Lulu has been given her own private office—not a cubicle, because Gates believes that everyone needs a quiet place to "think about things." Lulu's office is precisely the same size as every other office in the building, with the exception of the occasional vice president, who gets a little more floor space. Lulu has a window, a desk, a computer (possibly two or even three computers if she is developing programs that must work on different operating systems), and a big "whiteboard" mounted on the wall where she can scribble notes and diagrams, then erase and revise as necessary. She quickly discovers that Microsoft places enormous emphasis on electronic mail—E-mail—and that messages, questions, and answers blink up suddenly on her computer screen at any time of the day. When she is working on a new program and has a question, she simply taps a few keys and instantly her question is blinking away on ten or twenty screens throughout the company. Typically the responses come pouring in within minutes. At Microsoft, they call these fast responses "flame mail," multiple messages that come flaming back at you, sometimes with friendly ferocity, but always with frank and concise opinions, information, and feedback.

One morning Lulu is sitting at her computer, staring at her whiteboard, when she has a nifty new thought about her program. She knows that Bill Gates is keenly interested in the project that she, along with dozens of other developers, is working on. And she would really like to know what he thinks of her new idea. So she turns to her keyboard and types the individual identifiers into the system: TO: BILLG   FROM LULUL. She follows this with two short sentences that describe her new idea. Ten minutes later her screen blinks. The billionaire company founder has a thought about her idea—and has sent back a one-sentence piece of advice. At Microsoft, can a $45,000-a-year employee *really* send messages to the chairman? I asked Gates this question, and he nodded his head enthusiastically: "Absolutely. If it's about our products, I *want* you to send E-mail to me!" He went on to say that you'll usually get his reply that same day.

To further promote this interchange of intellectual grist, the company frequently schedules weekend "Innovation Retreats." After being on the job for three months, Lulu is invited to one that will focus on the program she's been struggling with. A dozen or so people, software developers and marketing types, go off campus to one of Microsoft's retreat sites. Lulu's group goes to a big, rambling house on Puget Sound where they will concentrate on just that single problem. They arrive equipped with overnight bags, whiteboards, overhead viewer machines, and lots and lots of opinions and ideas. Gates is usually there, too, poking into everything and keeping the creative pot bubbling. There are formal presentations and informal small-group discussions, all directed at the featured problem. The chatter and crosstalk will cover not only how to design this new product, but also how the market might react to it and how best to sell it.

There is a looseness to the company. Jackets and ties are something of an oddity, while playing golf in the hallways on Friday evening is definitely condoned. Occasionally, Lulu has seen employees ride unicycles and stage jousting matches on the rolling green lawn in front of Gates's office. Everyone knows Bill isn't stuffy. He gets a kick out of watching these inventive contests from his windows.

In 1980, Microsoft was a tiny, struggling company with 80 employees. By 1991, Microsoft had over 5,000 employees and had become the acknowledged leader in the software industry. Do you understand why?

■

Countless multitudes of people on this planet struggle at some endeavor in order to scratch out a living. An incredibly tiny handful do that scratching better—much, much better —and amass great fortunes. Today these wizards are called billionaires. It takes enormous creativity to start with nothing and become a billionaire. But the basic game plan can always be summed up into one word: S.T.R.I.K.E. Within that game plan you must generate ideas, stay loose, make decisions and, with great energy and confidence, make those ideas happen.

Study well what the billionaire does. It may make you a millionaire.

Afterword

THE PAYOFF

Sometimes life seems to conspire against us. We want to make a big, important creative change in the way we work or live, but the day-to-day, itsy-bitsy stuff keeps piling up in front of us ("As soon as I get these few things done, then I'll buckle down and really get cracking."). But, of course, that pile of itsy-bitsies will always grow faster than our ability to whittle it down. The human mind, conditioned to be scared stiff of real change, naturally resorts to the insidious and debilitating *Mañana Defense*. "I'll think about that tomorrow."

You now have a powerful weapon to employ against the *Mañana Defense*. The simple six-step process called S.T.R.I.K.E. will give you a direction that you can, and should, begin to head toward today. S.T.R.I.K.E. will set your idea-making into motion. Ideas will begin to cascade out of your brain. You will be able to pick the best one of those ideas to carry forward. You will triumph over the *Mañana Defense*, and with courage, joy, belief, confidence, and enthusiasm you will make that idea happen.

■

Think about this: A single new idea can potentially change your life. No one else is in charge of your life. No one else will force you to think up that elusive idea and then make it happen. *You* are the single person who cares most passionately about you. So get started today.

Be creative.

Generate a new idea.

Then make it happen.

You may discover that accomplishing an original idea is the most exciting and rewarding thing you will ever do.

And it only takes one.

Acknowledgments

I would like to acknowledge the people who—through the years—helped to make this book happen.

- My father, Alfred Emmerling, who showed me the love of drawing,

- My uncle, Gordon McAlpine, who showed me the excitement of selling,

- My first boss, Hanley Norins, who showed me the power of enthusiasm,

- My last boss, Dick Manoff, who showed me the path of the entrepreneur.

I would also like to acknowledge my children, Samantha and Jonathan, who contributed ideas that I shamelessly appropriated for this book. At Simon & Schuster, I am indebted to senior editor Fred Hills, his associate Burton Beals, and trade division president Charlie Hayward. And thanks to my agents, Artie Pine and Richard Pine (a father-and-son act) who were energetic cheerleaders from the very beginning of this long, wonderfully complicated process.

To the innovative people I interviewed in person—usually staying far longer than they had expected—a sincere thank you. The list includes Sir Peter Ustinov, Stephen Sondheim, Dr. Lee Salk, John Akers and T. Vincent Learson of IBM, Bill Gates of Microsoft, Don Petersen and Jack Telnack of Ford. Others who were generous with time and creative thoughts: Jill Barad of Mattel, Anne Busquet of American Express, Peter Diamandis of Diamandis Communications, John Evans of News Corporation Ltd., Fred Gluck of McKinsey, Professor Reese Jenkins of the Edison Papers, Dale Lang of Lang Communications, Marshall Loeb of *Fortune*, Allen Paulson of Gulfstream, Don Peppers of Perkins/Butler, Max Pine of Restaurant Associates, Peter Rogers of RJR Nabisco, Mickey Schulhof of Sony, Harold Simmons of Valhi, John Symons of Gillette, and Al Ueltschi of FlightSafety. I also wish to thank George Bremser, Jr. of ETAK, Gael Greene, restaurant critic and author, Bill Shephard of Creative Education Foundation, and Remar Sutton, columnist and author.

To the friends and associates who aided and abetted: Lesley Alderman, David Beattie, Steven Begleiter, Russ Berman, Gerry Byrne, Joe Campanella, Edgar Cullman Jr., Bill Curry, John Donoghue, Peter Eldredge, Jed Falby, Bill Garvey, Art Gilmore, Jim Guthrie, Robert Hannan, Steve Harris, Jim Hayes, Gene Klavan, Wayne Lachman, Carol Taber, Ray Sachs, Clare Hamm, Ed Higgins, Charlie Hess, Sue Lehmann, Luis Ortiz, Alan Pesky, Nancy Soohoo, Carl Walston, Jim Waugh, Giboney Whyte, Sandra Woodson, Elliot Zaref, and Dick Zorn.

Finally, effusive thanks to the public relations professionals who actually returned my phone calls when I was requesting nearly impossible "executive floor" interviews: Bruce Bond, Glen Bozarth, David Fausch, Howard Geltzer, Paul Pruess, Marty Taucher, Barbara Taylor, and Peter Thonis.

About the Author

John Emmerling has earned his living for thirty years by generating ideas. Born in Detroit, he attended the University of Michigan and paid most of his expenses during college by selling cartoons and gag lines to greeting card companies. An award-winning advertising copywriter, he is currently president of the advertising agency that bears his name, John Emmerling Inc., as well as an instrument-rated pilot, scuba diver, and avid skier. He lives in New York City.